I Paddled My Own Canoe

by
Stephen A. Lusch

Enjoy reading the true stories

Steve Lusch

Order this book online at www.trafford.com/08-0508
or email orders@trafford.com

Most Trafford titles are also available at major online book retailers.

© Copyright 2008 Stephen A. Lusch.

All rights reserved. No part of this publication may be reproduced, stored in a retrieval system, or transmitted, in any form or by any means, electronic, mechanical, photocopying, recording, or otherwise, without the written prior permission of the author.

Note for Librarians: A cataloguing record for this book is available from Library and Archives Canada at www.collectionscanada.ca/amicus/index-e.html

Cover photo: the author on the Laiard river near Fort Simpson, NWT in 1973.

Printed in Victoria, BC, Canada.

ISBN: 978-1-4251-5877-4

We at Trafford believe that it is the responsibility of us all, as both individuals and corporations, to make choices that are environmentally and socially sound. You, in turn, are supporting this responsible conduct each time you purchase a Trafford book, or make use of our publishing services. To find out how you are helping, please visit www.trafford.com/responsiblepublishing.html

Our mission is to efficiently provide the world's finest, most comprehensive book publishing service, enabling every author to experience success. To find out how to publish your book, your way, and have it available worldwide, visit us online at www.trafford.com/10510

www.trafford.com

North America & international
toll-free: 1 888 232 4444 (USA & Canada)
phone: 250 383 6864 ♦ fax: 250 383 6804
email: info@trafford.com

The United Kingdom & Europe
phone: +44 (0)1865 722 113 ♦ local rate: 0845 230 9601
facsimile: +44 (0)1865 722 868 ♦ email: info.uk@trafford.com

10 9 8 7 6 5 4 3 2 1

TABLE OF CONTENTS

Introduction
Acknowledgments

Runaway Boy	1
Innocent Until Proven Guilty	4
The Duck's Tail	8
All Things Being Equal	12
I've Got A Headache	16
A Trapper's Life	18
Summer Vacation	21
Things I Regret	27
Scared Bears And Boys	29
Dead Cat Tails	33
How To Drive Your Teacher Mad	39
The Smoky River	43
Alaska Or Bust	53
Bachelor's Club	60
Homesteading - Marriage - Mosquitoes	65
Moose Tails (one and two)	68
The Great Pig Caper	83
Pigs - Final Episode	87
Bear Tails (one and two)	90
Squirrel Dog	100
Horse Tails	103
Cow Tails	113
Curiosity Almost Killed The Cat	121
The Bird Dog	125
My Own Trap Line	128
Murphy's Law	136
Unsolved Mysteries	141
Almost Famous Athletes	146
Marriage Is Built On Love, Trust and Respect	150
About The Author	154

INTRODUCTION

How do you explain to someone why a seventy year old man flatly refused to grow up? My wife has been struggling with this problem for a long time. She is no closer to an answer now than she was forty years ago! Could the reason be as simple as a desire to live in the past? Was it the dreaded mid-life crisis, or perhaps his second childhood? The answer is none of the above. I simply find it more pleasant to recall the past than to worry about the future. I will leave the worrying to the politicians. After all, that's what they get paid for. I would prefer to spend my time thinking of the humorous things that happened 'yesterday.' It's a strange phenomenon, but looking back, some of the worst things really weren't all that bad. In fact, some of them were downright humorous.

One good example of this took place on a cold November evening in 1937. That night a large stork flew over my parent's modest home in Cody, Wyoming. It dropped me off like so much excess baggage! As if this wasn't enough, a mean old midwife picked me up by the heels and slapped me smartly! on the bottom. Then she handed me to my bewildered Mother. I was angry! I let the world know it by screaming at the top of my lungs. This went on for a few minutes until I opened one eye to see if all my crying was accomplishing anything. I was amazed to see my Father and two older sisters standing there with silly grins on their faces. It was at that precise moment I decided that crying wasn't working. Then and there, I made the decision to devote my life to humor. I have found it works fairly well. A good sense of humor will make a hardship a lot easier to endure. An amazing thing happened when I stopped my bawling and smiled back at them. They all laughed in return. My Dad began dancing a little jig around the birthing bed. I thought, "Man alive! If a smile could cause so much pandemonium, what would a burst of hearty laughter do?

In reading these stories, there are a few things I want the reader to understand. Namely: My stories are all true, with just a little "adorning" here and there to spice them up. For instance: When I am telling about how cold it was, I want you to know the mercury in the thermometer did not actually lift the corner of the cabin off the ground. Nor did the words that came from our mouths actually freeze. But it truly makes you understand that it was bitterly cold! Also, it may have been an exaggeration to say that it took four mosquitoes to carry a grown man away. However, they were VERY big! When you read about my wife, please understand that I wasn't quite as uncaring as it sounds. Admittedly, she was overworked and underpaid, but so were we all. The truth about my parents is that they were the most loving and caring people anyone could hope to meet. I did get disciplined fairly often, but rest assured that I deserved every bit of it and more. (There were plenty of my little escapades that they never learned about!) I never once questioned whether or not I was loved. Truthfully, I was loved more than I deserved. As for my 'pesky' sisters, I am amazed to see how much they matured in later years. Please don't tell them, but I am quite proud to have them for sisters. Even "MagPie" (MayJoy) is a lot easier to get along with!

If you should read anything in this book that you consider an impossibility, perhaps it can be attributed to what is called "adorning the truth." If you are still unhappy with it, you can write to me. Better yet, why not write your own book? At least, don't let it stop you from reading the remainder of these truths!

Should you get the idea that I love the life I have lived, you are absolutely right! I think the generation that I have grown up with has been truly blessed. Our generation lived in an era when people still worked with horses. They advanced from there, to a man actually walking on the moon! It was during our lifetime that space stations came into existence, as well as many other unbelievable achievements.

Up until I turned fourteen years of age, I lived in Cody, Wyoming. It was then my parents moved to Northern Alberta to a small town approximately two hundred miles north of Edmonton. It was a big change for us, and very exciting for me in particular. I loved every bit of the pioneering aspect of things. I'm sure my Mother missed running water, indoor plumbing, electricity and natural gas heating, but she never once complained. Dad and I felt we were right in our element.

After Wilma and I got married (in Oregon) I brought her to Alberta where we started our life together.   In Oregon, it was unusual for the temperature to fall below zero. It was near the end of November of 1960, and the change must have been quite a shock for her. I recall a remark she made, one extremely cold day, as we were driving to town. She said she couldn't see how people could survive in this weather! But survive we did! We actually began to enjoy even those cold winter months. One thing I liked was that she snuggled close to me to stay warm. She doesn't do that anymore. Perhaps it is because of better heating systems?

Within five years, we had four children. Sandra was born in 1961. Stephen followed in 1962. Then, to round it off, our twin girls, Rebecca and Brenda arrived in 1966. This was quite a handful for someone with my rambling nature. Wilma found it difficult too, and especially so, since it was before 'pampers' were invented.   By now we had discovered what was causing all these births. It was due to Wilma's direct orders that the stork quit visiting our place! We are extremely proud of our children. Fortunately, they did not inherit my wander lust. I do, however, take credit for their good looks.

One day at a family get-together, our Son, Stephen suggested that I write some of my adventures down. That way, our Grandchildren could enjoy them and gain an understanding of what life was like in the "olden days". I enjoyed writing them; and as I did so, I began emailing them to the kids. They, in turn, shared them with their friends. I certainly didn't expect the response that I got as a result. Emails began arriving from as far away as Kansas. They all wanted to know when a 'book' was coming out. Here at last is the first installment. I hope you enjoy it!

ACKNOWLEDGMENTS

This is one of the hardest parts of my book, because so many people have encouraged me to put these stories down on paper. I know I'm going to miss some of you, and for this I apologize in advance.

First of all, **my children** have reminded me of things to write, and many times when I had lost my inspiration, they encouraged me to continue. At times (most of the time) I had notes and papers scattered all over my office. I know this was a sore trial for my wife, Wilma, who is a neat freak. Yet she rarely complained, as long as I kept the door to my office closed. She also tried to keep me from any exaggerations in these stories. She did a marvelous job of this, and I truly thank her for her perseverance and encouragement.

My Father passed away in 1979 and my Mother in 1987. This was before I had even started thinking about writing a book. Somehow as I embarked on this journey, I always felt they were there cheering me on. My Mother began teaching back in 1924 and taught in several one-room schools; both before and after she met my Father. She always wanted me to take more of an interest in scholarly pursuits, but I was a dreamer. I've always wished I had been born a hundred years earlier. I wish she had lived to see this day. I am sure she would have been happy. I believe I owe her a great deal of credit for this effort.

Credit also goes to my good friend, **John Doroshuk** from Rocky Mountain. House, Alberta. Many times he got on my case about putting some of my stories down on paper. John is a life-long Missionary and has spent many years in the Ukraine and Russia, working tirelessly to bring the good news of Christianity to the people there. John had intended to write a part of the introduction. However, when I finally got ready for publishing, he was gone on another missionary journey. I will probably have him do one for the next installment. He is the same age as I am and should probably be thinking about retirement. However, as far as I know, he has no such plans.

Vonda Johnson of Valleyview has been a tremendous help with printing pictures for me on her computer. Thank you, Vonda!

I cannot forget those friends who provided the actual source of many of my stories. To name only a few: **The Campbell boys, Arne Johnson, Art Adolphson, Terry Johnson, Peter Flanagan** and all my **classmates** who got me into so much trouble!

Finally, I owe a great deal of gratitude to my sister, **Ramona Johnson**, who has probably been my greatest supporter over a number of years. She has worked tirelessly, typing the manuscript to the proper format for the book. That entailed correcting spelling and punctuation errors etc. She has had papers spread all over her home, trying to get things sorted out and in the right order chronologically. I know she has more than likely done more work on this than I have. I should mention her patient husband, Jim, who could have resented all the hours she spent working on this project, but didn't. Without her help I'm sure this wouldn't have gotten completed. Many thanks, Ramona.

Our Children: Sandra, Brenda, Rebecca and Stephen

Me with "Scottie"
(My parents either had Scottish Terriers or St. Bernards.)

Age six

Me on "Buck"

My "three" sisters and "Laddie."

Mom and me

Barbara, Steve, Ramona

RUNAWAY BOY

My childhood years were spent in Cody, Wyoming; a place where tales of Frontiersmen were rampant. We had a neighbor by the name of Bradford, who was a real 'honest to goodness cowboy.' Also there was an old man named Mr. Stilp who lived in our bunkhouse. These two guys found a ready audience with me and, of course as a young child, I believed everything they told me. I realize now that some of the 'stuff' they declared as truth, was in fact pretty far fetched! I didn't care, and I lived their wild adventures right along with them. In fact, in my mind, I even made them more extravagant than they really were. One thing the good Lord blessed me with was an active imagination. I admit, I let it run wild at times.

With that in mind, it was fitting that my life ambition was to become a mountain man; a man who spent his life blazing trails, living off the land and enjoying the good life of hunting and fishing. I envisioned myself tramping through the wilderness with only a skinning knife, my trusty Winchester and a pack of necessities. These necessities included salt, fishhooks and coffee - even though I didn't drink coffee until I reached the lofty age of twelve! Coffee was one thing a mountain man must have in his pack! We lived on a small ranch, so of course I would have a horse to ride and another for packing needed supplies and game. It was a wonderful fantasy and I still like it. This wonderful dream still remains, but at seventy years of age, time has pretty well passed me by.

I might have achieved this ambition except for one drawback. Until I was twelve years of age, I had all kinds of terrifying visions of vicious animals roaming the sagebrush around our place. I admit I never saw any of them in the daylight, but at night I knew they were there! In fact, I seemed to hear them prowling around me as soon as it got dark. Sometimes I saw their eyes glowing and their wicked teeth gleaming in the darkness.

At one time a cougar had wandered in close to our settlement and killed a little boy. So, I knew there were cougars out there just waiting for me to get careless. Mr. Stilp had enlarged on this true story with some added tales of his own close encounters with cougars and other wild animals. When I had to walk home from Cub Scouts at night, I was sure they were slinking along behind me! I kept swiveling my head around so I'd see them before they got me.

At the tender age of nine, the pressures of civilization got to be too much for me to bear. I decided to run away from home. I knew my parents would stop me if they knew my plan. That was mainly because of all the valuable 'work' I did around the place! (You need to know that I had three sisters whose only ambition in life was to make my life miserable!) It would serve them right if they had to take up the slack. I laid my plans well. By four p.m. I was ready! I had all I would need to survive: three peanut butter sandwiches, a pocketknife, a couple dozen matches, and a stout cord to make a bow with. My plan was to get far enough away by the time darkness fell, that I couldn't change my mind and return home. Everything went according to plan. I left a note where my Mother would find it.

I had actually gotten about three miles out in the brush when it got dark. I didn't want to light a fire the first night, in fear it would be spotted, and I would be forced back into slavery! I hoped to reach a cave that the Campbell boys and I had found previously. There I would 'hole up' and wait for Spring! It was already October and the nights were getting cold.

Of course the cougars were closing in! I could hear them prowling around, along with a pack of wolves. My nerves were tighter than a bow string! From my hiding place, behind the sage brush, it seemed I could see the tip of the mountain lion's tail twitching. Suddenly a coyote (a real one) let out a series of yips and howls just a few yards off. The details are a bit vague in my memory after that, but suddenly a great force unleashed within me. I was gone like the wind! I easily beat the 'four minute mile' and had at least three minutes to spare! I found myself shinnying up the cottonwood tree by my bedroom window. The plan was to slip quietly into my room, get a good nights sleep, and sneak out again in the morning. No one would be the wiser. I had very little life or breath left in me after that run!

Suddenly, as I was climbing though the window, my Dad and little sister stepped out of the darkness and grabbed me! My heart nearly stopped! I might have escaped, even then, but my running shoes were already smoking and I simply couldn't get any traction! It was just like I was spinning my wheels!

Humiliation was the order of the day. My sister, whom we called "Magpie," kept breaking out with her annoying laughter. It was almost more than a nine year old could bear! My freedom had been sweet - but very short lived! Twenty four hours later, my pulse was almost normal again, and I could begin planning my next escape.

Part of my punishment, of course, was to apologize to my Mother. We both cried a little and I decided that life at home wasn't as bad as I had thought it to be! I stayed home another fourteen years. As I look back on it now, I wish I could go back home again!

INNOCENT UNTIL PROVEN GUILTY

My parents were very practical people and didn't try to confuse us with stories of Santa Claus or Tooth Fairies. We always knew where the Christmas gifts came from; but that didn't make it any less exciting. As for tooth fairies, it wasn't hard to tell the difference between a fairy and my dad. I remember the first time I had a loose tooth. I was standing down by the barn. Dad sauntered up and 'innocently' asked if he could have a look at my tooth? I obliged by opening my mouth, and the next thing I knew, my tooth was on the ground! It hadn't really hurt, but I thought there could be no harm in yelling a little. It worked so well that Dad gave me a dime.

Dad had a very soft heart, but he could not resist playing pranks when the opportunity arose. One warm day I had gotten up the courage to climb up on our horse, Buck. He was so named because he was a buckskin gelding; not for his 'bucking' ability. I had climbed up and was laying down on Buck's broad back, just day dreaming. I was dreaming about being a cowboy and was actually starting to doze off. That was when Dad spotted me. He sneaked quietly over and smacked Buck on the rump. Buck was just as startled as I was, and he leaped right out from under me! As fate would have it, there was a pile of fresh cow manure right where my face was destined to connect with the earth! I'll admit, some pretty wicked thoughts began to run through my mind. Dad would have been surprised, had he been able to see into my little blonde head! He tried to apologize, but it was pointless from someone who was almost rolling on the ground laughing. (Him of course!)

One of the first Christmases I can remember is when I was five. At that age, my biggest regret was that I was not an Indian. Therefore, I was extremely pleased when I opened my gift and found it to be a bow and arrow set. Granted, the arrows were fairly blunt, but in light of how they seemed to veer off course, it was probably the best thing. Dad had made the set himself and it was pretty powerful for a boy my size. I was given a lecture on being careful where I pointed it. "Even though it was a toy, it was still a dangerous weapon." (Yes, Dad. I know.)

Now remember, it's Christmas Eve. "Eve" being short for evening, which means it was dark outside. I was told that I had to wait until morning to go hunting or target shooting. I had observed that when my little sister wanted something badly enough, she would screw up her face and whine. Of course my big old Daddy would cave in and get it for her! I wanted to shoot my bow in the house! Since this method had worked so well for MayJoy, I thought "Why not give it a shot?" I began the whining process, slowly building up volume and complaining that "MagPie got to play with her doll in the house. It just wasn't fair!" Unbelievably, it worked! I made a mental note to try this again sometime; as I began to see all kinds of possibilities for the future.

Dad cleared the furniture away from one end of the living room and set up a plywood target. He thoughtfully told my sisters to stand behind me while he showed me what to do. After a couple tries, I got pretty good at it. Then the girls wanted to try. All three of them placed their presents out of harms way and joined the fun. Barbara and Ramona shot a few times and it seemed they were having more fun with my bow and arrows than with their own gifts.   Dad even got in on it, as he was just a big kid at heart. Magpie, who was about three and a half, placed her new 'store bought' doll on a box at the far side of the room so she could have a shot at the target. She really didn't have the strength to do much, but she insisted on a turn. Beings she was the baby of the family, she usually got her way!

Finally I saw my chance and snatched it away from her and let it fly. The arrow seemed to have a mind of its own, and swerved across the room directly at her new doll. It went in one side of the doll's head and came out the other! It just sat there quivering. Had the doll been the target, it would have been a perfect shot. I'm telling you now - and it was the truth then (sixty five years ago,) It was an accident! My three sisters all said that I had done it on purpose; and of course the 'baby' still blames me after all these years.

In light of that accident, it seemed nothing short of a miracle that Dad bought me an air rifle when I was eight. My instructions went something like this: "Now Steve, this is a dangerous gun and if I so much as hear of you pointing it at anyone, I will take it away from you and wrap it around a tree! **"Do you understand me?"** "Yes, Dad. I promise. Trust me!"

This was a promise I intended to keep, even though the temptation to try it out on my sisters was great. I vowed I wouldn't give in to that temptation.

Sometime later, my cousin, Arnold Lusch, and I were playing in an old car graveyard at the bottom of our pasture. We were having fun shooting at the glass in the windows of the old vehicles. In those days they didn't have safety glass and little circular pieces of glass would pop out when you hit them. This was a lot of fun, but eventually we drew a bull's eye on the side of the barn and started target shooting. Arnold made the remark that my gun wasn't much of a gun, because it barely made a dent in the barn wood. I didn't like the way he was insulting my gun. One thing led to another until it evolved into a full-scale argument. Finally, I challenged him to a test to prove how powerful a gun it really was. Arnold was to take ten steps ahead, bend over and let me shoot him in the rear end. This put a different light on the subject, and he tried to weasel out of the experiment. However, I shamed him into trying it. Reluctantly, he agreed and paced off ten extremely long steps and bent over. I was prepared, so before he could change his mind, I plugged him in the bisquit! I was really surprised that my cousin could jump so high and so quickly too! It was nothing short of amazing! If only we had owned a video camera in those days, I could have made a fortune. I must admit though, that the screeching was a little nerve racking. The jig he was dancing was most interesting. There didn't seem to be any particular beat to it, but it was extremely fast!

Then Arnold did the unpardonable. He headed for home to tell my Dad! I knew if Dad got wind of this, I was going to be in a lot more pain than Arnold was. I pleaded with him until he relented .. but on one condition! I had to let him shoot me in the same location. After witnessing the antics that he had gone through, I wasn't too keen on it. He assured me though, that there was no room for bargaining. Not only that, but I had better make up my mind quickly before he changed his! I was beginning to sweat as I paced off fifteen long steps and bent over. And would you believe that heartless scoundrel made me retreat five steps! I actually think the anticipation was worse than the pain, and the pain was sheer torture for a few minutes. He actually had the audacity to try for a second shot, but I was moving too fast for him to get a good aim, and he missed! At any rate, the day was saved, and I got to keep my gun awhile longer. We have remained good friends even though most of the years we have lived about a thousand miles apart. Maybe it was better that way, because the combination of the two of us did seem to spell trouble! It was mostly his fault, of course!

About a year and a half later I made the most amazing shot of my career. I was in the pasture shooting at tin cans when I saw my oldest sister, Barbara, standing up beside the house. One hundred yards might not be far with a modern rifle, but remember, this was a B.B. gun. I pumped it up and aimed way over her head and pulled the trigger. I wish I hadn't done it, but wishing doesn't alter the fact that I did!

Maybe if she hadn't been so 'bossy'; but being the oldest child made her think she had the right to boss her little brother around. I suppose it may have caused a wee bit of resentment. I think I was more surprised than she was when I scored a direct hit! The way she carried on, you would have thought she was mortally wounded. I had hit her dead center of the south end, if she was walking north, and on her right cheek. I tried pleading with her, even working up a few tears, but all my efforts fell on deaf ears. As soon as Dad came home, I knew the jig was up and made a run for it. However, like all criminals, I coudn't resist returning to the scene of the crime. I was captured and hauled before the Judge, Jury and Jail Keeper! (These were titles my Dad held.)

First of all, I had a date with the razor strap; then a trip to the cotton wood tree, where Dad proved he was a man of his word. He literally "wrapped my gun around the tree!"

I was an old man of ten before I got a single shot 22 rifle for Christmas. Dad took me aside and said, **"Son, this is a dangerous weapon. Don't ever point it at ...."** "Yes, Dad, I promise."

Have you ever heard that old proverb about what the road to Hell is paved with?

MayJoy and Steve

Steve gives lessons on the proper use of his new bow and arrow set.

THE DUCK'S TAIL

The injustice of it all hit me on that balmy Spring day as I came in from the pasture. My Mother had three girls hanging around the house, doing nothing most of the time. It seemed to me that I was given all the hard chores. I decided to rebel and sneak away the first chance I got. I found that wasn't easy, with my little sister, Magpie, always spying on me. Not only that, she always wanted to tag along. She thought boys had more fun than girls and I think she secretly wished she was a boy. I had to be very careful that she didn't learn about my plans.

After finishing the milking, and bringing the pail of fresh milk into the house, I managed to get her involved in taking care of it. In the meantime, I phoned the Campbell boys and asked them to meet me at the foot of the hill. We would explore the hills about two miles east of our place. Previously, we had discovered an ancient Indian grave above a sand cliff. After rainstorms, we sometimes found blue colored beads that had washed down to the base. This was a spot where we could day dream about 'olden days'. Sometimes we chose sides and played "Cowboys and Indians." For some reason, I always wanted to be an Indian and I always did away with a lot of cowboys!

It was my lucky day because I got away undiscovered. When the Campbells showed up, we had the whole glorious day ahead to spend however we chose. In the process of being imaginary mountain men, we came across a little water course named Sage Creek - or 'crik', depending on what mountain man we were pretending to be. We started wading in the creek in search of excitement. We smeared mud over our faces and splashed around to cool off as we worked our way downstream. Suddenly a mallard duck flew up near our feet and nearly scared us to death. It was a hen who had been sitting on a nest. In the nest, we found seven eggs. This potential food reminded us that we had left home without lunch. Suddenly we felt hunger pangs. It was mid-afternoon by this time and the more we thought of eggs, the hungrier we became. In my imagination I could even smell Mom's fresh homemade bread and cinnamon buns, which were probably cooling on the sideboard right now.

Let me deviate a little here and talk about hot, homemade bread. Just the aroma of it could make a thief out of an otherwise honest boy or girl. Mom didn't have enough individual bread pans, so she often used a large cake pan and baked several loaves together. When separated, one end of the loaf was left open.

When Mom's back was turned, one could reach in and snatch a small handful. This, of course, left a hollow in the loaf. No one would be the wiser until she went to put them away. I want to make it very clear that my angelic sisters were just as guilty as anyone when it came to being bread thieves! It is impossible to describe those cinnamon buns. They were simply mouth watering. For some strange reason, when Mom went to put them away, their numbers had always diminished. This was a mystery we didn't work too hard to solve. However, I will make this simple observation: Who could hang around the kitchen and avoid suspicion easier than my sisters?

Vanilla pudding was another mouth watering concoction Mom often whipped up. On one occasion, I was doing my imitation of an Indian sneaking up to scalp an imposter, when I spied an extra large bowl of pudding. A large spoon stood erect in the bowl. No one was guarding this delicious looking bowl of temptation and it was just begging to be sampled. It didn't have to beg for long. I reached stealthily through the door, grabbed a spoonful and made for the great outdoors; spoon in my mouth as I made my escape. I came to a screeching halt when my taste buds reacted to a terrible deception! It was homemade soap instead of pudding! I had already taken a swallow before the enormity of it all hit me. Wouldn't you think one would have a sign up telling what was in the bowl? I protested, between gagging and choking, but couldn't arouse the slightest sympathy from anyone. For two days everything I ate had the taste of soap. I even began to sniff at genuine bowls of pudding after that. I also had to endure taunts from my 'sweet' sisters like, "How would you like a nice bowl of pudding, Steve?" (All three of them could be very sarcastic.) Enough of this! Let's get back to the duck!

The eggs reminded us that we were hungry. We gathered them and wrapped them in our shirts to carry home. I know that some animal rights activist is going to accuse me of being cruel. But think of it this way: How would you like to be the hen and have to sit on eggs in the hot sun day after day? I can imagine that duck was already regretting whatever romantic impulse had been the cause of her laying those eggs! We had actually done her a big favor. Now she could swim or fly around without a care in the world. Single again, she didn't have to worry about her children growing up to be juvenile delinquents. If you feel sorry for her, wait until you hear "the rest of the story!"

When we arrived home, Mom suggested that we put the eggs under a setting hen to see if they would hatch. Momentarily, we forgot our hunger and soon had converted the dog house into a nursery. Soon we had the hen installed on the eggs and as proud of them as if they were her own. She must have thought she was "Super Hen," because the very next day all seven eggs hatched. She had a family of the strangest looking baby chicks she had ever seen. Aren't children supposed to resemble their parents? Where did these chicks inherit their flat beaks and webbed feet? I am sure she began to question the parentage of the rooster, but she loved those babies anyway. She did her best to raise them like chickens should be raised.

It so happened that an irrigation ditch ran through our yard. When the ducklings discovered that, they waded right in and began to swim and quack. The poor hen was really upset, but she waded out after them as far as she dared. She squawked at the top of her lungs, trying to persuade her babies to get out of the water. Of course they didn't obey, causing her to spend much of her time running up and down the ditch bank. She was baffled as to why her chicks wouldn't scratch and cheep like normal chicks should. At night, Chickens turn in early for a nights sleep. On the other hand, ducks enjoy late nights and like to paddle around until it is fully dark. There seemed to be a serious difference of opinion and lack of communication here, and it was never settled. Mother hen would just about have them coaxed up to the dog house when one of the ducklings would make a break for it and head for the water. She even went to the extent of trying to swim herself -- which was a miserable failure! After a couple times of nearly drowning, she gave up on that.

It's a good thing that poultry grow up quickly, because I fear she would have given up on motherhood and become a lesbian, had it taken any longer. Fortunately, both stepmother and ducklings survived, and the hen was wanting to set on more eggs. Perhaps next time it would work out normally. Certainly she would check the rooster's background out more thoroughly!

We had to clip the duck's wings when they got older, but when Fall came they became more difficult to catch and didn't get clipped as often. They began to fly around, but they always came back. As wild ducks began to migrate, our ducks sometimes followed for awhile; then circled and came back. Finally, the ungrateful things took off with a wild bunch and never did return! I watched for them the following Spring but apparently by then they had decided they preferred being ducks.

I recently watched a movie about penquins. I'll tell you one thing for sure: I wouldn't want to be one of them! A duck lives a life of luxury compared to a penquin!

There is an old saying that goes,"You can't change a leopards spots." It is equally true that you can't make a duck into a chicken, or a chicken into a duck! I've also heard that love is blind, and after observing humans,I have come to the conclusion that this is true as well. I'm sure there is a deep truth buried in these proverbs, but you'll have to search it out for yourself. I've done my job!

This is the end of THE DUCKS TAIL!

ALL THINGS BEING EQUAL

I feel like I must agree with the famous gun fighter, Bat Masterson, when he stated that he thought most things evened out in life. "Take 'ice' for example. "The poor get it in the winter and the rich get it in the summer." He apparently wrote this on the evening of his death, as it was discovered on his typewriter the next morning.

I recall an unpleasant time when I was about ten years old. I was loudly proclaiming my innocence, hoping my father would have a change of heart and not give me the spanking he thought I deserved. However, much to my disappointment, my pleas fell on deaf ears, and he went ahead with my punishment. Dad stated that although he was not one hundred percent sure of my guilt, one thing he was certain of. That was, for every time I had received a punishment while innocent, he was sure that I was guilty of several that had gone unpunished. He figured it all evened out in the end. At the time, I heartily disagreed with him, and even though I knew he was right in his assumption, it didn't stop me from screaming about the pain.

*** ***

One time on the farm, I happened to spy a skunk going into the chicken house. I had been forbidden to shoot the 22 rifle without an adult present, but this seemed like the time to get some target practice and perhaps become a hero as well. My mother had stated that a skunk had been stealing eggs and she wanted to see him stopped. I rationalized that she would be so grateful to see the skunk dead, that she would overlook my transgression. I still believe all would have gone ahead as planned, if only I had waited for the said skunk to exit the hen house <u>before</u> I pulled the trigger. However, hindsight being better than foresight, I went ahead and plugged the little critter while he was still inside. Worse yet, in the excitement I managed to gut shoot him, which was a big mistake. He expired all right, but before he did, he managed to liberally spray the entire chicken coup, making it impossible to breathe in there. The chickens all moved out and began roosting outdoors, as well as laying their eggs wherever they thought they were hidden. This performed the dual purpose of making their eggs harder to gather, while at the same time, making it easier for other skunks to steal them.

Somehow my mother took offense at this. As we were walking to the house she (with a switch in hand) posed the question as to "what I thought my punishment should be?" I suggested that a suitable punishment might be 'not allowing me to eat cooked turnips for two weeks or longer.' She was fairly unreasonable and asked for more suggestions. I then offered to keep the wood box for her cook stove full for a month. This might have worked out, but she said that this was already my chore, so she turned that idea down too. I tried several more which she rejected. Then she asked me "What does your school teacher do for punishment?" I reluctantly told her that he made us bend over and hold our ankles while he gave us 5 swats across the rump with a switch. (Not that I had any firsthand knowledge of this procedure, or course!) She scoffed at me and told me that I was so clumsy that I couldn't even bend far enough to grab my ankles. Thinking to prove her wrong, I bent and grabbed both ankles. Suddenly I felt a sharp burning pain on my bottom and before I could get my wits about me, I felt 2 more! I will admit I had been pretty stupid, but not stupid enough to stand around and wait for more! As I was speeding away, holding my posterior, I looked back to see a broad smile on my mother's face as she tossed the switch into the irrigation ditch. I had to admit that the idea of bending over while she had a switch in hand, was enough to earn me the 'stupidity award'! I deserved that one. Later, when television made it's debut, there was a program called "The Beverly Hillbillies," in which Granny used the same tactics with Jethro. He never seemed to get wise either.

*** ***

I won't go into detail about the many deserved punishments I received, but I have to be honest and admit that I got away with many indiscretions where I should have been punished. In the long run, they did eventually even out! In fact, I did have first hand knowledge of the above described punishment in school. Somehow, with a great deal of luck, I managed to keep that little secret from reaching the ears of my parents, or the scales would have tipped the other way. The policy of my parents was that if you received a spanking in school, you had another one coming at home! Only at home, it was much harder. Sometimes parents can be so unreasonable!

*** ***

Ron Doroshuk shared a story with me that merits passing on. It took place when he and his older brother, Walter, were about ages ten and twelve. During harvest it was their job to haul the grain from the combine to the granary and unload it. This of course took several trips. It was a long reach to the clutch and brake pedals for Walter. He had to pile some coats on the seat so he could see over the steering wheel. He was managing quite well, when Ron begged to drive. His begging was so pitiful that Walter gave in and let him try. Because Ron was shorter yet, he was unable to steer and still reach the clutch and brake at the same time. He still managed to get the truck up to about 40 mph on the sandy road. Suddenly it started to swerve from one side of the road to the other. Ron couldn't reach the brakes and the end result was that they ran into the neighbor's fence, sheering off a fence post. The post flew into the air and came through the windshield. Upon arriving back at the combine, Dad Doroshuk immediately spotted the big hole in the windshield. He was not at all pleased! Ron was sure he would receive a whipping, and went sobbing to his dad, laying his face against his chest. He confessed his guilt and must have done a good job of it, because Dad Doroshuk grabbed Walter and gave him the whipping. Needless to say, Walter couldn't understand the justice in this at the time. Now that he is a father, I believe it makes more sense to him. I don't think Ron asked to drive again for a long while though.

*** ***

When I was about six years old, my sister, Ramona and I were clowning around, just play fighting. She picked up a hammer that happened to be laying close by, and swung it, pretending to hit me. Unfortunately, it slipped out of her hand and hit me in the head, knocking me dizzy. I began to scream and dance around, holding my head and generally making a lot of noise. Dad came running out and asked me what happened. So naturally, I told him that Ramona had hit me in the head with the hammer. He didn't ask any questions. He just grabbed Ramona and began to give her a severe spanking. Now I knew, even at age six, that Ramona would never purposely hurt anything, and especially not her favorite little brother. I began to yell at my Dad that "she didn't mean to hit me...it was just an accident." Dad just dropped Ramona and picked me up and finished up on me. At the time, I thought it was totally unfair that I got punished at all. After all, I already had a severe head ache! However, now that I have raised four kids of my own, I can understand Dad's frustrations. Sometimes in spite of the best of intentions, a parent can easily make the wrong decision.

*** ***

When our twins, Rebecca and Brenda were small, they were so identical that it was easy to mistake one for the other. One warm spring day they carried an ice cream bucket full of dirt into the bathroom where they proceeded to make mud pies in the bath tub. Of course their mother caught them at it, and seeing the terrible mess she would have to clean, thought a spanking was in order. She grabbed Rebecca first and was educating her, while Brenda tried to beat a hasty retreat. Of course Brenda was already crying in anticipation of the pain she knew was headed her way. Wilma dropped Rebecca, who tried to scurry away behind her. She mistook one for the other and grabbed Rebecca and proceeded to spank her again. Rebecca was screaming, "Wrong one! Wrong one!" Wilma never realized her mistake until my Dad, who was over having coffee with us, brought it to her attention. Of course this -- when he was able to stop laughing. The girls were about three years old at the time.

*** ***

Sometimes life just seems unfair when the unpleasant things pile up. But if we can make it through the bad times, things will eventually even out.

I'VE GOT A HEADACHE

There was a small stream that ran behind our house in Cody, Wyoming. Two or three big cottonwood trees grew beside its bank. This set the scene for another of those things "I wish I hadn't done."

The stream, or ditch, was only about 5 feet across, but if you used your imagination, it could become a raging river. At any rate, the stream provided a lot of entertainment on a hot summer day.

I had just been reading a book about Tarzan. (We didn't have television then). I came up with the brain wave of swinging from branch to branch by strategically placed ropes. Starting high up in the tree, you could swing from limb to limb until you would finally swing down to the ground - or into the creek! I got pretty good at this monkey business, swinging through the tree, making ape sounds. (I made the sounds, only when my sisters weren't around to hear me!) I guess I'll have to blame it on over-confidence, or else something distracted me. Somehow, on that fateful day, I missed the last rope, swinging about 15 feet to the ground. Naturally, I landed with my head hitting the root of the tree! There seemed to be a brilliant explosion of light, accompanied by little colored stars spinning around in circles, plus a loud roaring in my ears.

I figured I was in the process of dying. Now, I had a great fear of dying because, even though I wasn't a bad kid, I was quite certain I wasn't going to make Heaven. I wasn't looking forward to the other place. Just the previous Sunday, the evangelist at church had looked right at me and declared, "Repent of your sins or you will never make Heaven!" I realize now that he probably wasn't looking at me intentionally, but at the time I was certain he had meant me and only me! Regardless, I had put it off to a later date, and now I thought it was too late.

When I was finally able to scramble to my feet, I ran into the house screaming, "I'm dying! I'm dying!" I had expected some sympathy, but none seemed forthcoming. When my parents saw the quickly growing knot on my head, they did get concerned, but my three sisters just giggled. Dad assured me that I was going to live, which was a big relief to me. Now I could postpone that little thing about repenting. I had a headache for two or three days after that.

It wasn't more than a couple weeks later that I missed the school bus going home, so I just fooled around the playground until it began to grow dark. I ran as fast as I could for home, taking all the shortcuts I knew. I wanted to get there before the dreaded darkness closed in on me.   As I was going top speed through someone's back yard, my adams apple made abrupt contact with a clothesline! Again I experienced those colored stars circling around, as I lay on my back gazing up at the sky.   Do you suppose it was another reminder about that 'repenting thing'?

Anyway, these are just a few of the many times I have "wished I hadn't done that!" I suppose there will be more.

A TRAPPERS LIFE

I used to dream about becoming a trapper when I was about knee-high to a tall horse. Just thinking about it got me through many a boring school day. A typical afternoon in grade school would find me staring off into space, building a log cabin or paddling down some wild river. I envisioned monster fish jumping around my canoe. Sometimes the teacher would be standing in front of my desk when I came out of my trance. She had that frustrated look on her face, like she was wondering how she would ever reach through the insulation surrounding my brain! I had some excellent teachers, but they had no idea what an impossible task they had set their minds to. I remember Miss Bell (my first grade teacher) waving her hand in front of my face and saying, "Steve, where are you?" Of course I couldn't tell her I was miles away on Rattlesnake Mountain.

One morning in June, I decided to play hooky and hide up in the hills behind our home, where I loved to explore. I had a problem though. I had three nosey sisters who delighted on tattling on me. We had ridden the bus to school, so I loafed around the bus stop until they had gone into the school. Then I made a hasty retreat. I walked a half mile out of town and lay down in a dry irrigation ditch, intending to stay there until the coast was clear. I waited for the court house clock to strike ten, but something must have gone wrong with it. It seemed like I had been there for hours; and that time was standing still. This adventure didn't seem like much fun, with no one to share it with. Then the idea struck me. "Why not sneak back to the school yard at recess and talk my friend, Dean Campbell into coming with me?" Finally the courthouse bell tolled ten. It was working, after all! I ran back to the school, only to find that Dean was spending recess in the Principal's office for some misdemeanor. Now I was in the same fix as before. Why couldn't my friends stay out of trouble! Just as I was turning to leave, I felt Miss Bell's hand on my shoulder. The jig was up. I started stammering excuses for being late. But "SHUT UP, Steve!" She hadn't even realized I had been absent. My Dad had phoned the school and wanted me to come home and help rake hay in preparation for stacking. Wow!! I had almost told on myself, when the impact of it all hit me!

Had I not come back to the playground around the time Dad phoned, he would have learned about my playing hooky. The punishment would have been much more painful than what Miss Bell would have given me. Maybe someone 'up there' was looking out for me after all!

If there was any kind of work I did like, it was driving the tractor. I appreciated the opportunity to make my sisters envious. I loved farm work as long as it involved a steering wheel and a motor! Dad had taught me to do jobs like raking hay or harrowing when I was barely able to reach the clutch pedal. My sister, Barbara, thought she was a better driver, but I knew she wasn't.

Mom was a school teacher and she thought I had the ability to be a straight "A" student. She wasn't too pleased about Dad keeping me out of school. Later on that evening, I heard her getting on to him about it. I was supposed to be asleep in my room upstairs, but when I realized they were talking about me, I put my ear down on the heat vent in my room and listened in on their conversation. Mom was saying, "Bill, Steve is not doing as well as he should in school and I hate to see him miss any more." Dad replied, "I know the boy needs education, but right now the hay is drying out and I can't find anyone to work. Besides," (now get this one) "Steve is as good on the tractor as any hired man. I promise I won't keep him out any longer than I have to." I jumped up so fast I almost brained myself on the bedstead and had to bite my tongue to keep from whimpering. I made myself indispensable around the hay field so Dad wouldn't hire someone else. I am ashamed to admit that my head may have gotten a little swelled after that compliment! In those days it was a common thing for farm kids to be kept out of school during busy seasons.

SUMMER VACATION

In mid May, when school let out, it seemed like a great load had been taken off my shoulders. Summer loomed ahead and September seemed an eternity away. Camping, fishing, and just plain old goofing off was the order of the day. My Mother had a rake and hoe with my name of them. She suggested in the strongest sense that I put them to use in the garden and try to keep the rust off them. Dad also had a list of chores for me, including keeping the wood box full and bringing the cows in from the pasture for milking. Sometimes I thought they must stay up all night thinking of things to keep me busy. However, I found that with a little ingenuity and a lot of luck, I could still sneak away and indulge in all kinds of more worthwhile pursuits. This usually involved the four campbell boys. If we put our five little heads together, we could always get into something that would cause the adults to shake their heads in exasperation. They wondered if we would ever survive until we were old enough to leave home!

I had one serious problem though. It was my little sister, whom we all called "Magpie." Her real name is MayJoy. She wanted to tag along on all these misadventures and we didn't want any girls to be a part of our gang of cutthroats. If I managed to escape, Magpie ran straight to the Folks, and tattled, saying I had gone away without finishing my chores. They and my two older sisters hunted me down, and it was back to 'slavery' again! It seemed to me that those 'lazy' girls never had to do anything but make my life miserable. They always accused me of being spoiled because I was the only boy in the family. I didn't see it that way at all! I wondered why a bolt of lightening didn't strike them down for their wild exaggerations.

In Cody there was, and still is, a rodeo every evening in the summer. There is also a 'western-style' parade down the main street. During the month of July, games of chance and cotton candy booths etc. were set up down town. There were also tents where Gypsies plied their fortune telling skills. One of the most exciting things to me though, were the fire works. In Wyoming in the late 1940's, there were no laws concerning how powerful the firecrackers could be, so there were some powerful ones sold.

My friends and I used to save every penny we could through the month of June to spend on fireworks in July. It was loads of fun to see how high a tin can could fly; or one might drop a lighted 'cherry bomb' behind an unsuspecting friend to see how high he could jump.

One morning a young boy (who shall remain nameless, even though the statute of limitations had run out) lit an entire package of firecrackers and threw them under the flap of a Gypsy fortune teller's tent. It sounded like a war was going on in there! You'd never believe how many people came streaming out of that tent. They were speaking in another language, but it was easy to understand what they meant! I think what upset them the most was that some of their small children hadn't gotten dressed yet.

The Campbell boys and I were having a great time blowing things up, when someone threw a cherry bomb over the fence into the chicken pen. A big hen grabbed it up in her beak and was running away, trying to keep it from the others. Then it blew! It took her beak right off and she lay unconscious for a few minutes. We were standing around, planning her funeral, when she jumped up and continued staggering around the pen, apparently thinking the other chickens were still chasing her. She couldn't peck things off the ground anymore, but learned to 'scoop' grain up. She lived for the rest of the year, until Mrs. Campbell turned her into fried chicken for one of our camping trips.

THE CIGARETTE CAPER

Mr. Campbell smoked "Camel" cigarettes. The whole family was always after him to quit, but to no avail. Mrs. Campbell was constantly drilling us boys on the evils of smoking, until we vowed to help her with her husband's 'filthy' habit. There was a slim-line firecracker called a "Ladyfinger." We hit upon the ingenious idea of loading up some of his cigarettes with Ladyfingers. Surely this would encourage him to stop smoking. We convinced ourselves that we were doing him a big favor, and that he would probably thank us for being so caring. The idea was acted upon immediately. We removed a little bit of the tobacco - then shoved the firecracker, back into the middle of the cigarette. We then tamped the tobacco back into the end. We did this so carefully to several cigarettes, that no one could tell they had been tampered with. When Mr. Campbell came home from work, he washed up, came into the living room and sat leisurely back in his chair. He pulled out a cigarette and took a deep drag. He was just reaching for his newspaper when the excitement began. It wouldn't have been so startling, had the firecracker not been so far into the cigarette; because when it blew, it also blistered his lips. When he had first come home, he was calm and relaxed. Now there was nothing calm nor relaxed about his behavior! He grabbed the first kid handy and took off his belt, putting a few blisters on his

22

behind. He continued until he had done the same to all five of us. We were afraid to run from him.

Exausted and out of breath, Mr. Campbell sank back into his chair. He pulled out another cigarette and lit 'er up. We all sailed out the back door at top speed and headed down to the river, where we stayed until everyone had gone to bed. We hoped things might cool off a bit on the home front, or at least he'd be in a better mood. We thought we heard him calling us, but the river was making quite a bit of noise, so we weren't sure. The sad part was that it never stopped him from smoking, though he did check his cigarette packages very carefully after that episode.   Because of his 'ungratefullness', we quit trying to help him.   About two weeks later he took us fishing with him again. Maybe that was his way of saying "thank you." He just didn't know how to put it into words!

"PHEW!!"

It was on this trip with Mr. Campbell that Dean and I took their Cocker Spaniel along. As we looked for arrow heads out in the sage brush, we had a great time scaring up Jack rabbits for the dog to chase. The dog and we boys were intent on our various pursuits when a skunk moved out in front of us. Natually, the sensible thing to do seemed to 'sic the dog' on it. The dog was more than willing, but it proved to be a bad idea! Suddenly, the dog began to whine and dig its' nose into the dirt. It carried on something awful! The dog seemed unable to see, so Dean and I rushed in to rescue the poor thing. This proved to be another bad idea because the skunk still had a little scent left and it graciously shared it with us!

We finally found our way back to Mr. Campbell, which proved difficult, as the dog seemed to have lost all sense of direction. She kept plowing furrows in the dirt with her nose. Worst of all, Mr. Campbell didn't seem overjoyed to see us either. The first insulting thing he did was to toss us into the river. As if that wasn't enough, he made us ride back home in the back of the truck We actually preferred this because it would have been very stuffy with six bodies in the cab. It was almost like we had Leprosy or something! On arriving home, we jumped out and ran in the front door, only to have Mrs. Campbell chase us right out the back door! At this point we didn't feel like anyone really loved us. Mrs. Campbell finally came out with a bucket of warm, soapy water. She made us strip down to our birthday suits and scrubbed us until we hardly had any skin left. Then we were sure nobody loved us! She left us standing out there naked while she hunted up some clothes for us to put on. The other kids just stood there and laughed at us in all our humiliation. That kind of thing can scar a sensitive person, like myself, for life.

When I finally got home, my own loving family even avoided me; standing upwind of me for a few days. Here's a little proverb you might find handy sometime: "Smile and the world smiles with you. Get sprayed by a skunk and you stand alone."

NEIGHBORS, AND PARTNERS IN MISCHIEF

Campbells had an acreage that fronted on the main highway between Powell and Cody, Wyoming. Their large, two story house sat back from the highway behind a small apple orchard. When these trees were in bloom, the aroma was just heavenly. Behind their house, the land sloped back to a big garden and then a pasture. About a quarter of a mile below that was the Shoshone River.

All this was watered by an irrigation ditch that flowed along the highway and was then diverted down to both the garden and pasture by a smaller ditch. I'm describing all this to set the stage for the next little scenario I want to share with you.

THE PAUSE THAT REFRESHES

One summer's day, the driver of a large Coca Cola truck lost control and rolled over right in front of Campbell's place. It landed about six feet from the irrigation ditch. While the driver walked back to town to get help, all us kids (including the girls) worked liked beavers tossing bottles of coke into the ditch. They floated from there down to the pasture. A couple of us were employed down below, pulling bottles out and stacking them where they could be retrieved and put to 'good use.' Coca Cola had a motto that said "The pause that refreshes." All of us did a lot of refreshing after that. The coke went real well with the sweet rolls and cakes that we had found in the garbage behind the town Bakery.

We boys were strolling down the alley one day when we discovered this bonanza behind the afore-mentioned bakery. They threw out any baked goods that were more than a couple days old. Now, before you start wrinkling up your nose and rolling your eyes in disdain, let me explain. These pastries were all wrapped in celophane and stacked out back in boxes. They were actually very clean. However, just mention that they came from the garbage and people begin to get an image of flies and all kinds of nasty things.

A few weeks after we had made this amazing discovery, my mother was drilling me as to why I seemed to have lost my appetite? I felt I must tell her about all these baked goods that I had been indulging in. She demanded that I bring her some so she could check my story out. I went out back where they were hidden and brought in some of the best ones. Mom realized they were clean and still soft, so she confiscated them; putting them in her pantry.

I had been careful not to disclose all my stash in case of some upcoming emergency -- like running away from home or something. That very evening some friends dropped in unexpectantly. Mom didn't have anything to serve with the coffee, so out came the sweet rolls and other goodies. The company was delighted and remarked how delicious they were. It was then my little sister, Magpie piped up and exclaimed, "Yes, and would you believe that Steve found them in the garbage!" (It was nice to see someone else in trouble for a change! You may have guessed that MayJoy came by the name 'Magpie' because of her chatter!) Mom's face was red for a week and she had quite a time explaining it to our friends. However, they seemed to think it was funny, and kept right on eating. It wouldn't surprise me if they didn't drive down the alley on their way home! Sometimes too much pride will make you go hungry.

HIM OR ME? IT'S YOUR CHOICE

One problem Dean and I seemed to have was that we always liked the same girls. That made for a few times that we would get into fights. We'd say things like *"I don't ever want to see you again!"* However, it wasn't long until we were playing together, having forgotten the whole issue. Now, these 'girls' were blissfully unaware of our affection for them. We wouldn't have had the nerve to talk to them anyway. One day we decided to settle all this dissention and let the girl decide. We planned it all out. We would approach her and let 'her' choose between us! The object of our affection was a cute little brunette named Charlotte Mullens. She had long curly hair that hung almost to her waist. Dean and I each picked a bouquet of apple blossoms and went down the street to learn who would be the lucky suitor. We stuttered and stammered around until she finally understood what we wanted her to do. She graciously accepted the bouquets and then ... she dropped the bomb shell! She didn't like either one us and thought we were a couple of hillbillies! We were happy with the compliment, but brokenhearted with the rejection! It took us nearly 15 minutes to get over our heartbreak.

We consoled one another with the fact that it had been 'her great loss,' and after all, there was always Veronica! Veronica would have been second choice anyway, but by now we had lost our nerve. Instead, we made a pact to leave girls out of our lives altogether. They say, "The road to Hell is paved with good intentions," but we meant it when we said it.

Many years later, another long-haired brunette named Wilma stole my heart and I fell all the way to the altar!

WELL, SUMMER IS OVER, SO I MUST CLOSE THIS DOOR!

THINGS I REGRET

"I wish I hadn't done that! I wish I hadn't said that! Lord, if you will help me out of this mess, I'll be more careful in the future." These are just a few of the phrases I have used over the years, when I had gotten myself into a jam that I couldn't seem to squirm out of.

All of these lines were running through my mind as I walked through the snow on that November afternoon. I was on my way back to the school from my band class. In my exuberance at being released from band practice, I had gathered up a big handful of snow, formed it into a hard packed snowball, and released it into the air. It had come down in a perfect landing on the back of Clifford Russell's head. It couldn't have been more accurate if I had aimed there; but I hadn't. When the furious Russell demanded to know who had done it, I had a problem denying it was me, when about thirty of my classmates were pointing their fingers at me.

If I had picked anyone to hit, Clifford Russell would have been the last guy I would have chosen. His Dad had enrolled him in the local Golden Gloves boxing team the previous year, and he had built quite a reputation. I, on the other hand, knew nothing about fighting, and didn't want to take any lessons that day! Clifford, of course, figured I had intentionally nailed him and was demanding that we settle the score then and there. We were circling around with our fists up. All the blood thirsty little sixth graders were egging us on, yelling advice, as if they wished they were involved. Right then I sure was wishing they were - and not me! At that precise moment, the band teacher walked up and separated us. I was hoping it would end there, but some wise guy hollered, "Meet him after school and settle it!" Clifford agreed, so to save face, I was reluctantly forced to meet him behind the band house after school.

The remainder of the day was agony for me, as I tried to figure a way to get out of this, without letting everyone know how scared I really was. It was one of those times when my brain was "frozen in space." I couldn't come up with anything. At four o'clock, the final bell rang. All I had to do was sneak off, or face up and take a licking. I wasn't happy with either choice, but picked the latter, because no 12 year old wants to be called a chicken.

When I arrived behind the designated building, there was already quite a crowd gathered. There was a lot of talk about how

Clifford was going to 'make mincement' of me - plus other gruesome descriptions of what I might be facing once Clifford arrived. To prolong my agony, Clifford was late. I think he was late on purpose. Eventually he did arrive with a group of his admirers. The crowd made a circle around us, making me wonder if all those kids could find nothing better to do than stand around and watch me get beat up! You can see, I was just overloaded with confidence! Clifford hadn't been expecting much of a contest, but I had made my mind up that if I was to get killed, I wasn't going to make it easy for him. While he was prancing around, waving his arms in anticipation of an easy victory, I dove in like a small whirlwind. Wonder of wonders - I wound up on top! With my arms and legs wrapped around him in a death grip, he was unable to squirm free.

The fickle crowd soon changed their chants in my favor instead of my opponents! I was elated and tried to pretend like it hadn't been an accident. Clifford was so mad at being humiliated, that he began to cry. This was my undoing and I began to wish that I could let go and let it end right there. I did give into that wish -- released my hold -- acting as if this were a warning of what would happen, should he dare ever challenge me again! It was then that I said, "I wish I hadn't done that!"

Everything went down hill from that point on. I limped home that night with a bloody nose and numerous bruises, not to mention a bruised ego. However, on the positive side, I was a lot wiser.

Another amazing thing happened that day too. A cute little girl by the name of Darlene Harkens, stayed behind and tried to clean up my bloody face with her handkerchief. I was amazed at how quickly the pain seemed to disappear, especially when she whispered that she thought I was "cute." Then, for some strange reason, she ran away. Kind of the story of my life!

SCARED BEARS AND BOYS

I was born near the end of the Great Depression, and my Dad was struggling to support a family of six. That required a lot of hard work just to make ends meet. He was used to hard work, having grown up on a farm in Nebraska with his 13 brothers and sisters. It didn't leave a lot of time for recreation. My parents made every effort to see that their children had the opportunity to enjoy camping, fishing, picnics and any outdoor activity available. In my case, this was easily accomplished with my good friends and next door neighbors, the Campbell family.

Campbells had five boys. Four were close to my age, and were some of my best friends. The oldest, Bernard, was in his late teens. They also had three attractive girls. However, as boys from age nine to twelve, we considered girls nothing but a nuisance.

The four younger boys and I used to torment Bernard until he would chase us down and beat the daylights out of whomever he could catch. The name "Bernard Campbell" was a name that invited trouble. His bedroom was on the second floor, with a long staircase to the main floor. At one time there had been a stove in his room and the stovepipe hole still remained. The five of us little monsters would stand outside his room and yell, **"Barnyard Cowbell..Barnyard Cowbell,"** along with some other choice poetry. Our voices carried through that stovepipe hole. (They called us "The Hole in the Wall" gang!) As far as I know, our poetry was never published, but it was delivered at the top of our lungs and was designed to drive him crazy. When Bernard reached the boiling point, he would burst out in a rage, with homicide on his mind. He'd take his frustrations out on the one unlucky guy he caught. Of course we were prepared for this and didn't make it easy for him. We were smart enough to know that the odds of escape were four out of five. (Remember there were five of us.) But woe to the one out of five who was snared! Bernard was absolutely merciless, and we knew it. Still we could never resist the temptation and did it over and over. I was faster than the others -- something like a raging monster coming up behind you lends wings to your heels! Because I got away most of the time, I never suffered like the younger ones did. They sported a few bruises much of the time.

I often spent the night at their place, and one thing they had a shortage of was beds, so we were all packed into one or two narrow beds. That was fine if you got an outside position, but it was torture by asphyxiation for the guy who wound up in the middle of all those sweaty bodies.

Mr. Campbell worked for the Husky Oil Refinery. He loved to fish and spent a lot of his spare time doing so. He was, without question, the greatest fly fisherman I have ever known. One of his greatest virtues was that he often took the five of us boys with him. Maybe he did this to give Mrs. Campbell a break.

I'll never forget the first big fish I caught. It was on the North Fork of the Shoshone River. I was about eight years old. Immediately after I had cast my first fly out, a four pound Rainbow chomped down on it. In my surprise and excitement, I gave a mighty heave and the fish went flying over my head, landing in the willows. I followed it up the bank and literally pounced on it; afraid it might somehow get back to the water. Mr. Campbell laughed so hard I was afraid he would choke.

THE TRAGIC LOSS OF MY BEST FRIEND

When I was eleven years old, my closest friend, Dean Campbell, was drowned on a school outing. Our class had gone by bus to the Hot Springs at Thermopolis, Wyo. We were paired up for safety reasons. Naturally, Dean was my partner. He went out of the building to the outside pool without me noticing. After awhile someone came running inside with the news that someone was laying on the bottom of the pool. I had the premonition it was Dean, and it was soon verified. I felt that it was my fault, and I have never experienced sorrow like that in my entire life. I dreaded the eighty mile trip back to Cody. I thought I would be the one who had to break the news to his parents, but of course the school officials had already done that. I was let off the bus at the driveway of our farm. Dad met me and just held me as I sobbed my heart out. I was afraid the Campbell family would hate me; but of course they were very understanding and let me know they didn't hold me accountable. Two or three years later, Mr. Campbell passed away and the boys and I became closer than ever - if that were possible. I thought I would never get over it, but youth is a great healer.

Life eventually got back on track and we soon went back to tormenting Bernard. The odds were down now though; it was three out of four.

YELLOWSTONE PARK and BEARS

After living in Canada for a couple years, I got the opportunity to spend two weeks back in Cody with the "Hole in the Wall" gang. Mrs. Campbell arranged a camping trip to Yellowstone

30

for the whole family. By this time, I was fifteen, and the Campbell girls were beginning to look a lot prettier. The trouble was, I wasn't bold enough to admit it to anyone, so us guys continued to make life miserable for them.

Campbells owned an old Buick that was missing a muffler, and pretty much all the tail pipes that went with it. When the driver took his foot off the accelerator, it would backfire and blow out puffs of smoke. We thought it was great fun.

When we arrived at the Fishing Bridge campground, all of us guys headed straight down to the lake with our fishing rods. It wasn't long before we had our limit of Cutthroat trout. Walking back to camp, we were all excited and talking a mile a minute; without a care in the world. In our absence, Mrs. Campbell had built a fire and was busy cooking a big meal for a bunch of hungry kids. While she was bent over the grill, a good-sized black bear padded up behind her and let out a sudden "woof." According to her daughter, Barbie, her Mom went about four feet straight up in the air and came down spinning, like her legs were a windmill. (Possibly a slight exaggeraton.) The bear took over, like he owned the place and was slurping the food up as though he had missed several meals and was trying to make up for it in one sitting! Mrs. Campbell hustled the girls into the car and fired the motor up like she was entering the Indy 500! When she let up on the gas pedal, there was an explosive sound, with an enormous cloud of smoke shooting out. This was more than Mr. Bruin had bargained for and he .lit out of there like he was on fire; or like he had just remembered a previous engagement elsewhere!

The problem now was that the bear headed down towards the lake, and on a collision course with four unsuspecting boys! Got the picture? He burst on the scene with another startled "woof" and we all scattered like a bunch of quail. Well, all except for Jim! Jim threw both his fish and pole, and was fifteen feet up in a four-inch Lodge Pole Pine before gravity set in! He began to slide down, digging both his fingernails and toenails into the poor tree. Eventually, he realized he couldn't hold on any longer and fell the last few feet to the ground. For awhile, he just lay there with his eyes closed. He was under the impression that the bear was still down there with it's jaws wide open. You have never heard such pitiful wailing as came from Jim's mouth that day. Of course we let him know that none of the rest of us had been the least bit afraid! After we gathered up all the fish and our gear, we went to the camp and ate everything in sight. We sure didn't want to anything for the bears! All night bears kept coming in to the camp,

31

but the old Buick was just fired up again. We'd all have a big laugh over it as we continued telling ghost stories to scare the sissy girls.

Do I look like an ornery kid?

DEAD CAT TAILS

My Dad and uncles are to blame for this little episode.   As a child I found it fun to hide under the table or some other piece of furniture. From there I listened to the adults rehash some of the mischief they had gotten into when young. Many an evening I would hear exciting stories of adventure, intrigue and narrow escapes experienced by my Dad and his six brothers. Some of the escapades were those of my many cousins and uncles; none of them sprouting wings! Dad's family lived on a small farm near Swedeburg, Nebraska. On a typical Sunday, with all the relatives congregating there, Grandmother Lusch often had to cook for forty people. I've been told that the more family she had, the happier she was. She was truly a remarkable woman. She died the year I was born, so I never got to meet her. I look forward to seeing her when I reach Heaven. I'm absolutely sure she is there now waiting for her clan.

I spent my early years in Cody, Wyoming, attending school through the 7th grade. I guess listening to a lot of these tales caused me to be just a teeny bit mischievous, even then. I slid through school just a few steps ahead of failure, but managed to pass each grade and move on. The amazing part of it all was that my teachers all liked me. After all, what is there not to like? I can remember more than one of my teachers saying that I was not living up to my potential. In fact, one assured me that I would likely become the president of the United States. I was, however, seeking a higher calling like being a cowboy or a trapper. I would accept the job of President only if there were no other vocations available.   I am sure I am to blame for many of the headaches my teachers endured, not to mention a few grey hairs.

I recall a time when I was in grade five. As usual, I had claimed a desk in the back of the room where I had more freedom to practice my mischief. Miss Dennis had some of the kids up front doing recitations. When she wasn't looking I would make faces at them and have them laughing so hard they couldn't recite. I was having so much fun that I failed to see the teacher move around behind me. Suddenly I was lifted right out of my seat by my hair. She threatened to send me to the Principal's office for some further education. I began to sob and explained that I had an uncontrolable ailment in which I would get seizures. They, in turn, caused my face to twist and contort out of shape. I felt very humiliated when the kids laughed at me.   She went to the front of the class and apologetically pleaded with the class to let her know if anyone else had any type abnormality that they could not control. She was so sincere that she had tears in her eyes. Those tears were my undoing. I couldn't help myself, so I stood up, and with tears of my own, confessed and admitted that I had lied; that I had purposely made faces to make the students laugh. She looked at me with her big blue eyes and I believe I saw both love and frustration in them. Her words were "Steve Lusch, I declare I'm afraid you are going to cost me my salvation!"

When I was 14, our family moved to northern Alberta, Canada. I went from a school of several hundred students to a one room school of approximately thirty. It ranged from grade one to eight. It was quite a change, I will admit, but we had a wonderful teacher, named Miss Turcotte. She really went out of her way to see that we learned something.

Things were a lot different now because Dad had gone from being a very successful building contractor to a missionary to a group of Ukrainian people in the hamlet of Forest View.

Having a preacher for a father was a totally new experience for me, and I was having a few problems living up to what the people in the congregation expected of me. My sister and I walked four miles one way to school when the weather allowed. In the winter, when it was too cold, the neighbors shared the dubious pleasure of driving us there with a team of horses and a sleigh, or caboose. The first winter there, the temperatures dropped down as low as minus sixty. In spite of weeks of continuous cold, we never missed a day of school. The school building was heated with a large barrel wood stove. The bigger boys had to split and carry the wood in each day. Miss Turcotte lived in a teacherage next door and went over at five a.m. to light the fire so it would be warm when the students arrived. About an hour before noon, the teacher placed a galvanized pail of water on the stove so we could all have hot chocolate with our lunch. Occasionally, at recess, some ornery boy would toss a handful of '22 shells into the stove for some excitement. It might take ten or fifteen minutes for them to explode, so by then we were all back in our seats looking quite innocent. It seldom fooled Miss Turcotte though. She would slowly look around the room of faces and see which ones were turning red. She usually picked the guilty party or parties. To begin with, my face turned red, no matter who had done it, but I found if I concentrated real hard on something else, I could get away with it.

One beautful spring day a group of us were walking to school and I found a bat that had gotten its radar system messed up, and was caught in a barbed wire fence. It was dead. It seemed such a shame the bat had expired without ever having accomplished any worthwhile purpose. I decided to see if perhaps we could get some purpose out of its death. Being of a scientific mind, I put it in my pocket and gave it a free ride to school. No one was in the school when we arrived, so I gently placed it in Miss Turcotte's pencil drawer. (Naturally, I wanted her to see it first before I showed it to the class). Strangely enough, it was late afternoon before anything happened, and I had actually forgotten about it. The warm gentle breeze drifting through the windows on that day, had caused most of us to fight to stay awake. We were eagerly awaiting for the final bell to release us from a day of hard labor. Suddenly, staying awake was no longer a problem. A deafening screech filled the air! It was enough to make ones hair stand on end -- which was a reality in Miss Turcotte's case. There she was, half leaning against the wall, her face was white and she had a look of horror in her eyes. She was trembling all over. Some of the younger kids had bolted for the exit. I wanted to join them as well, because it had just dawned on me what the commotion was all about. However, leaving might make me appear guilty. When she finally gained some composure, she pointed to the drawer and with stammering voice, said that a live animal was inside! Would someone volunteer to come and capture it? Seeing a golden opportunity to redeem myself, I volunteered. Of course the bat was still dead, and I carried it as nonchalantly as I could and tossed it outside. This caused all the little kids who had escaped earlier, to come tearing back inside! She looked at me like I was her hero!

After things had settled down somewhat, Miss Turcotte began the dreaded inquisition process. She looked around the room at each child. I began frantically to think of something else so that my face wouldn't turn red. This time, the process failed miserably and when she got to her former 'hero', she knew she had the culprit! "Why?" she asked me. I began sifting all possible reasons through my suddenly frozen brain. The only thing I could come up with on such short notice was "Science!" "Yes! I thought we should examine this bat as a science project and try to ascertain why it had hit the fence! Why had the bat's radar system failed?" I suddenly became "annointed" on the subject and had worked up a head of steam when I glanced upward into her eyes. I saw laughter there. She had outsmarted me again and was just waiting to see how deep a hole I would dig before

35

burying myself completely. She then dismissed the class - except for me!

We had a heart-to-heart talk. In this discussion, she told me that she was thirty one years old and this little stunt of mine had just taken an additional 15 years off her life. She had hoped that she could eventually get married and have children, but now she was afraid I had stolen even that from her. I assured her that she was a very attractive woman and that I would never have guessed her to be thirty one. I added, of course, that my only regret was that "I" was not old enough to become the lucky man. She then said something about a 'silver tongue' and hoped she was never desperate enough to listen to that kind of baloney! Miss Turcotte then patted me on the head and told me to head for home before she changed her mind and explelled me. I didn't let any grass grow under my feet! Oh yes, she mentioned, in passing, that I might expect her to come calling that evening to have a word with my parents. I lost great amounts of sweat as the evening went on. Every noise outside made me think she had arrived. (We didn't have telephones then, so she couldn't just simplify things and phone my parents.) At the slightest sound I would turn white and was getting some strange looks from Mom and Dad. This torture went on for several days until I finally wised up and realized it was part of the punishment. I am still amazed that my little sister (MayJoy) didn't tattle on me! I guess she was saving it until she needed a favor from me. She never guessed how much she could have gotten from me at that point!

When I began this chapter, my intention was to tell you about a dead cat. Somehow I got carried away, and some of you are wondering what the title was all about. Okay! Here goes!

Eventually I graduated from grade eight. Miss Turcotte, because of her 'great affection' for me, agreed to teach me grade nine if I would be willing to remain after school for one hour each day to learn algebra. Before I had a chance to answer, my parents quickly replied that "I would do that and that I would be glad to for the opportunity!" It was impossible for me to give my oppinion, with Dad's big hand over my mouth! So I let it ride. The ninth grade slipped by and after that we moved from ForestView to Valleyview. Valleyview had a two-roomed school, and I took two more years of schooling there. (That was the extent of Valleyview's education system at the time.) My parents agreed to take me back to Cody, Wyoming where I would stay with my sister, Barbara, and complete high school. This is where "THE CAT" enters the picture.

Barbara's husband worked for the Marathon Oil Co. They lived 20 miles south of Cody in an oil field called "Oregon Basin." I worked weekends in a gas station in Cody to make some spending money and money to buy gas for my 1950 Ford. In school, I chose to take "Band" and played the trumpet. This wasn't primarily to become a musician, but band students got to attend football games and cheer the team to victory. Each year the Band teacher took the students up in the hills for a picnic. Those who had cars were allowed to drive. I had to drive because I lived so far out of town. Barbara's neighbor had a daughter named Sharon, who was also in Band. She asked me very nicely if she could catch a ride home after the picnic. I could never say "no" to anyone, so I agreed to give her a lift home. This did present a problem, in that she was very attractive - and I was painfully shy around the opposite sex. Even though I was 16 years old, I would get tongue tied around girls and make myself look stupid. I know you are wondering how I could look stupid, but it's true! I attempted to solve this dilemma by inviting a friend named Bill Campbell to come with me.

The picnic was on Friday evening and ended about nine o'clock. Just as we came to the outskirts of town we saw a big orange cat that had been hit and killed by another vehicle. Bill suggested that we grab it and see if we might "play a joke on some unsuspecting sucker." (Bill's words). I already told you I had a problem saying "no," so we did it! On a corner of Cody's main street there was a little cafe, something like the ones in the sitcom "Happy Days". It was a place where all the young people congregated. We were stopped at a red light just in front of the double doors. The cafe was packed and bursting at the seams. Just as the light turned green, Bill opened the car door and heaved the cat, with some of its entrails hanging out. It landed in the crowd, which parted like the Red Sea in the story of Moses! I had to abandon the idea of treating Sharon to a coke, and instead put the pedal to the metal! We could hear the screaming and other unearthly sounds coming from the coffee shop from a block away. The owner happened to be close to the door and managed to get a fairly accurate description of my car, which was "dark gray, sporting a damaged trunk lid and a broken tail light." Almost immediately, the police car was after us, but by now I was a mile out of town and picking up speed all the way!

When we hit the turn off to Sharon's house, the police were gaining some. Sharon begged me not to lead them to her front door -- something about being afraid her dad might kill me! We sped on by, and took a dirt road out into the sage brush as fast as the old car could go. Suddenly, immediately in front of us, there was a wash out! It was about four feet deep and ten feet across. There was no time to hit the brakes! If you have ever watched the "Dukes of Hazzard" you will get the idea of what took place next. We landed on the other side; a little shaken up, but otherwise in good shape.

The police eventually decided they didn't want to risk it, so we were home free! Well -- we were 'free', but certainly not 'home.' It took us hours to find our way through the sage brush and around the wash out. The sun was just coming up when we pulled up to Sharon's front door. She said it was "the most fun and excitement she had had in all her sixteen years, and hoped we might do it again sometime!" I wasn't keen on trying it again! It seemed her dad wasnt either, so we just stayed good friends. Bill and I took all the back roads into town and sneaked into his parent's place. My cousin, Charles Quick, was there. He came running out and asked "Okay, what have you done now?" He said the police had pulled him over for a traffic violation and he could hear the description of my car going out on the police radio. "**..dark grey, damaged trunk, broken tail light...**" He was burning up with curiosity! We explained how we had innocently gotten a'foul of the law. Charles took us to a wrecking yard where I purchased a different trunk lid and tail light, which we quickly installed.

I rode the school bus for the next few weeks and tried to stay out of sight around town. My greatest fear now (as a grandfaither) is that my grandkids might read this and try something similar. I want them to know that "I was very lucky!"

I could have easily gotten into deep trouble, or even had an accident and have been the cause of someone getting seriously hurt. Anyway, my grandkids are ornery enough. I don't know who they inherited their mischievousness from - but it sure wasn't from me!

THIS IS THE END OF THE CAT'S TAIL!

HOW TO DRIVE YOUR TEACHER MAD
(IN ONE EASY LESSON)

Mrs. McQuade was really reading Agnes the riot act. Agnes Rassmusen was normally one of the better pupils, but the evidence was right there in her hands. The evidence, in this case, happened to be an old time alarm clock. This clock was supposed to be on the teacher's desk to announce recess, or the end of classes for the day. It happened about two o'clock on a drowsy Spring afternoon, when the sleepy class was jarred awake by the jangling of the alarm. To all appearances, Agnes was the guilty party. However, we all know that appearances can be deceiving. The most condemning evidence was Agne's face. It was beet red with embarrassment. The clock was in her lily-white hands! It was ringing, but it was the look of guilt that condemned her. Agnes was stammering out some kind of explanation, but in her current state, the words weren't coming out all that clearly.

Now, as Paul Harvey would say, you'll hear the rest of the story. There was a certain young man who sat near the back of the class, who had tip toed up to Mrs. McQuade's desk when she had her back turned. He filched the clock. Working quickly, so as not to be caught, he wound up the clock, turned and whispered "Agnes!" and tossed it to her, just as he pulled the alarm. What is a young lady to do? Allow the clock to hit her, or catch it? The answer is obvious and that is the picture the teacher saw when she turned around. Mrs. McQuade gave Agnes a short lecture and went back to her work at the blackboard. I sat 'very near' the young man in question, and the next thing I knew, a large eraser went zipping past my head, hitting the oil stove with a resounding "bong!" Again Agnes' face went beet red, which to the teacher was an admission of guilt. So Agnes got to listen to another lengthier lecture, which included a discourse on the proper behavior of a young lady.

I was in the tenth grade in the Valleyview High school, which claimed a total of two rooms. Grades seven and eight were in one room: nine and ten in the other. Mrs. McQuade taught grades nine-ten, a total of about thirty students. She was a good teacher, but almost too trusting of her students. As a consequence, her rowdy students were able to pull the wool over her eyes on a regular basis.

Valleyview was in the midst of an oil boom. The town was bursting at the seams with oil men from all over the country. We didn't have a drug problem in those days, but I was one of the few guys who didn't smoke. Quite a number of the girls smoked also. When the teacher's back was turned, one guy after another would get up and sneak away to the outdoor biffy to have a smoke. If there weren't more than two or three, Mrs. McQuade didn't seem to notice. If more that that disappeared, she would send me to get them back inside.

I actually began to resent the fact that they could take a break while I couldn't, so I began sneaking out too. One time, as I was making my secret exit, a younger boy was sneaking out the door of the other classroom. I grabbed him by the arm and swung him around in a circle, then released him back into his class. His momentum was so great, that he ran past his teacher at top speed, nearly colliding with some kids at the blackboard! The surprise was total, and when the teacher asked him the reason for his strange behavior, all he could do was stand there and stutter. I had gently pushed the door closed, so I could stand there and listen to his lame excuses. It took him at least a month before he could see any humor in it, and even then, he sought revenge for a long time!

The other teacher was Mrs. McCarol. She also taught a couple of our classes. At the beginning of the year, a bunch of us decided to give her phony names when she had roll call. As we were called upon the first day of school, we gave her our aliases. Each time the rest of the class would burst out laughing. The poor woman didn't know what we were laughing at, so she began to suspect that her clothes weren't properly tucked in, or something. She tried to look behind her to see if something was out of place. That just made us laugh all the more. Finally, in frustration, she got Mrs. McQuade to come in and check things out. It didn't take her long to weasel it out of one of the girls. The names and their owners were straightened out, resulting in most of the guilty ones being assigned to detention.

The local pool hall was a big temptation to a lot of the guys and that is where they hung out at noon hour. I had been taught that the pool hall was "a den of iniquity," so I stayed out of it. (This is not to say that I wasn't tempted.) One day, Art Adolphson and Ivan Rackiti got carried away in a game and missed the one o'clock class. They decided to continue playing until the afternoon recess in hopes that the teacher wouldn't miss them. Of course she did, and when they showed up, she stuck her finger in Ivan's chest and told him he "might as well go home if he couldn't be more prompt." Art thought this was just hilarious and he burst out laughing. She then ordered him to go home too and said she would "deal with them tomorrow."

I rushed over to Art's house after school and walked in without knocking. I caught them imbibing in some drink that certainly wasn't kool-aid. They looked so guilty that I burst out laughing at them. Then I proceeded to tell them that Mrs. McQuade was right behind me. You should have seen them scramble to get rid of the evidence! However, in their defense, I have to tell you that they said they only drank a "teensy weensy bit."

Bob Rasmussen had a stunt he liked to pull in the warm, sleepy afternoons when everyone was fighting to keep their eyes open. He would have previously wound the window blinds up as tight as they would go. Then when we least expected it, he released them. There was a wooden ball on the end of the pull string. When it banged against the window sill, it made a horrendous noise that caused everyone to jolt upright in their seats. Let me assure you, our eyes were wide open! He always got some detention for it, but he enjoyed scaring us so much that he didn't care.

You may have guessed by now that I thoroughly enjoyed teasing and embarrassing the gentler sex. What you probably didn't know, is that I was extremely shy and easily embarrassed myself - - if the prank was turned on me. Finally one day, the girls got their pretty little heads together and decided to turn the tables and get revenge. I suspect that Agnes was the ringleader. Anyway, as I was walking into the classroom after lunch break, two of them grabbed and held my arms, while the rest homed in on target and began kissing me. The surprise was complete and before I could escape and run, it was too late. I will admit that it wasn't entirely unpleasant. However, when the rest of the class, including my so called friends, erupted with laughter and cat calls, I surely wished I was anywhere but where I was! My face was crimson red and so hot you could have lit kindling on it. For weeks, all they had to do was smile and I'd turn red.

Nowadays I look at the kids from school and it makes me wonder what this old world is coming to. Then I think about how crazy we were and I realize there is still hope for the younger generation. I think, as a rule, the young people today are probably smarter and just as well adjusted as we were. I am glad though, that I lived in the times I did. We were a lot freer and there were less laws to live by.

Cars were a big thing then and every kid had to be a bit of a mechanic just to keep the old junkers going. I drove an old '41 Mercury and had picked up a set of musical horns for it. It only played four notes, so I was pretty well confined to one or two tunes. I've always been amazed that the townspeople didn't get up a petition against me. Suffice it to say, they just suffered in silence.

I didn't get straight "A's in school, but I have to admit that I enjoyed every minute of it. If I could live those years over, I believe I might concentrate a little more on education and less on nonsense. But then again --- probably not!

SMOKY RIVER

Steve Lusch - Art Adolphson - Arne Johnson

The Little Smoky River was a never ending source of entertainment for some of the young people in our community. In the Spring came the long awaited break-up, when the melting snow caused the water to rise, thus lifting the ice on the river. It was still fairly solid, but it broke up into large chunks. Some were large enough to make excellent 'rafts' for foolish boys to ride down river. We would go as far as the first bend where the ice blocks were forced onto the shore; allowing us a chance to jump off and run back to repeat the risky performance.

Some of these pieces of ice were very large - as much as 100 feet across. They were relatively safe to ride, unless the piece crashed into another and broke into several pieces. It sometimes happened that the impact flipped the ice over - or stood it on edge. One's options were rather limited in these cases and required quick thinking and action! Usually we could run and jump onto another block. But when that opportunity didn't present itself, we had to muster up extra energy and optimism and swim as fast as possible to another block. I mention 'swimming fast,' because swimming in ice water generally shocked ones senses into frenzied action!

I recall one occasion when Art Adolphson had to swim about a hundred feet to shore. Arne Johnson said "The water was actually smoking behind him!" I won't vouch for this, because Arne has been known to exaggerate on occasion. (More on this later.)

Looking back on this, now that I am older, smarter, and domesticated, I am amazed that one of us didn't drown. Tobias Johnson, father of the eight Johnson boys, often followed us down river. He tried to stay out of sight, but handy, just in case we needed rescuing. I am sure he prayed as he walked along. Most of our parents had no idea what we were doing, until after the fact. This river fun would last for two or three weeks. Each day the blocks grew smaller until they finally turned into what is referred to as "candle ice."

A group of us were at the river one Sunday afternoon, when a few six to eight foot blocks came floating by. I ran and claimed one that was reasonably safe. Arne took a flying leap and joined me. Our combined weight was maximum for the size of the block. By now the current had taken us about fifteen feet from the shore. The temptation for Art to join us was too much for him to resist. He grabbed a long pole and pole vaulted out to join us. With the extra weight and momentum of his jump, the block began to tilt. This caused the two of us on the low side to run for the high side. The block then proceeded to sink. This side show performance was repeated over and over until we were about a hundred feet from shore. None of us were eager to take a swim in the water, so there was a lot of pushing, shoving and perhaps some slapping going on! This action caused the ice to tilt a little more. Eventually, Art's momentum was too great. He appeared to just 'run off' into the river! (This is when Arne said that the "water was smoking behind him!") I don't remember the smoke, but I do recall that he swam with a great deal of enthusiam!

With one less body on the block, things settled down somewhat. However, the vision of Art running into the water, like he thought he could "walk on water" - combined with the expression on his face as he sank into that icy water, was so comical that I could hardly stand up for laughing! This lasted for just a short time, until I glanced behind me and noticed a wicked gleam in Arne's eyes. It didn't take many 'smarts' to realize that his evil intention was to kick me off too! I quickly remedied this by moving around behind him. His opportunity had passed! Arne said later that he really had to fight temptation, but he was afraid I might drown if he did shove me off the block. (I still don't believe him.)

Those were wonderful and carefree days and we thought they would go on indefinitely. I should add here that for Art to stay afloat was a miracle in itself, considering what he was wearing. He had on long underwear, a wool coat and work boots! But the fact is, that ice water seems to fill one with enormous energy for a short time. If you don't reach shore in the allotted time, you might be heaven bound!

As soon as the ice was almost gone, it was time for swimming and lazing around on the sandbar. There was a nice sandbar below Johnson's. The problem was, the best place to swim, was across the river. When the ice had all but disappeared, we swam across to the sandbar and let the sun thaw us out. It was at this time, one became sleepy from the warm sun, and dreaded the swim back across to home. We found that the best way to counteract this, was to run and leap into the cold water. This was an awful shock to the system, but not as agonizing as getting wet a little at a time. It wasn't long until the water warmed up, making it a very pleasant pastime. Each summer, 'Dad' Johnson's family increased considerably!

For a young teenager, in those times, the fishing was "unreal!" It was very easy to let it become an addiction. There were times we caught so many fish we had to string them on a pole and carry them between us. (This is not a 'fish story'!)

A favorite place to fish, was where the Sturgeon Creek ran into the Little Smoky River. Many that we caught, were in the five to ten pound class. It was a long walk in and out, but we had plenty of time. Sunlight lasted eighteen to twenty hours in the middle of Summer. These fish were locally called "Pickeral." There were also Jackfish, which I think are really called "Northern Pike." The Jackfish sometimes reached three to four feet in length. My Bro-in-law, Jim, caught one that was 47 inches long. He was ice fishing and caught it at Sturgeon Lake. It is mounted and hangs on his living room wall.

I recall one time being just a little bored. I took the hooks off a lure and lay down on a raft we had anchored in the middle of the river. I dangled the lure down in a school of pickeral that I saw lying in the shade underneath the raft. They came dashing and chopping down on this metal lure - shaking their heads like they wondered what this hard, tasteless piece of metal was! They tried it again and again. The saying goes that "small things amuse small minds." By lying flat with my face between a couple of logs of the raft, I could see it all very clearly. It became quite comical to watch, especially when two or more fish were after it

The raft (for diving) was anchored in the deepest part of the river. It was handy for poor swimmers like myself to rest upon when attempting to swim across. Our diving was not famous for gracefulness, but what we lacked in finesse, we easily made up for with enthusiasm. If high water took one raft out, it was no big deal to make another. The material was right at hand. Our rafts were not fancy, but they served the purpose. This river fun also kept us away from town; which seemed to please the town folk. They (the town folk), preferred having us do our mischief elsewhere. Also, if we were going to drown or break our necks, they didn't want to be responsible, and didn't want to have to clean up the mess.

The nearest hospital was over fifty miles away, over dirt or gravel roads. There were pot holes in this road so large, you could lose a Volkswagon in them! It sometimes took as much as four hours to drive the fifty miles, and that was when driving conditions were favorable. If it happened to start raining, you may as well be prepared to spend the night. We described road conditions as "Mud or Dust!" There didn't seem to be anything inbetween. Today, all major roads are paved and one can speed along at sixty or seventy miles and hour. But be sure to watch for 'frost heaves!' A big one can make you leave the ground for short distances!

Due to the trouble it took to get to a hospital, most injuries and sicknesses were left to home remedies. We were blessed with a district nurse at Valleyview. She handled anything that was very serious. The nurses were generally hard working, compassionate people. I'm sure they were underpaid, considering what they they had to put up with. There was one, however, who shall remain anonymous. She was extremely competent, but entirely lacking in what is called "bedside manners." One time she was working on a patient, a young man whose face had been torn up in a truck accident. As she worked on him, he asked her how bad his wounds were? She answered, "It's not going to hurt you for farm work." After that, whenever one of us got hurt, someone was sure to console them by saying, "Don't worry. It won't hurt you for farm work."

Somehow I seem to have wandered away from the "River!" Let's get back to it.

One early Spring day when most of the ice had melted, it left a roaring, muddy mess. A group of us boys were lying along the bank. We were having a competition as to who could tell the most fantastic, tall tale. It turned out to be a tie between some of the other guys. But the idea was hatched up about taking a boat and floating down river as far as the High Prairie bridge. It was about forty miles, as the crow flies. If we were to leave soon, we could get there and hitch a ride back before our parents missed us. However, we hadn't considered 'how crooked the crow might fly'. Anyway, in our simple minds, it didn't seem to be any great problem. Well - there was one small problem. You might call it an obstacle! This obstacle was called "Hell's Gate Rapids." It was a ten mile series of rapids. With the mention of these rapids, enthusiasm waned considerably. We had heard of four or five people who had drowned in these rapids, although we knew none of them personally. I was sure that with a little persuasion, I could count on Arne to take the dare with me. He was always game for an adventure. Besides, I assured him that with the water so high, "we would sail right through and hardly even feel the bumps." All the guys who weren't going were quick to agree that we two could make it. I've noticed, as a rule, folks who are not going to face danger, see no problem with it.

The boat wasn't a problem. Arne's older brother, Jim, had just purchased a dandy, homemade craft for the astronomical sum of ten dollars! Better yet, it only leaked when you put it in the water! Leaking wasn't a problem, someone suggested, because that was what God made coffee cans for...to bail with! Around a family of Scandinavians, you could always find coffee cans.

Because we were in a hurry, we quickly employed the younger Johnson brothers (without pay of course) to gather a burlap bag of carrots and turnips from Johnson's garden. On our way through town, we picked up a few loaves of bread, some pork and beans and my new 30/30 rifle. Two hundred squirrels had gladly sacrificed their skins that I might buy that rifle! We also took our fishing rods and tackle. Of course, we wouldn't be needing bed rolls because we only planned to be gone for part of the day. Duh!!

It was getting on to ten a.m. and the weather was hot and humid. The boat was stashed another five miles downstream and two miles from the end of the road. Arne and I were soon sitting at the road's end, facing a hot two-mile hike.   The thermometer registered 90 above. These were not the right conditions to inspire one to carry all that gear to where the boat was. But guess what! Just a few yards away sat an oil company's bombardier. (A bombardier is a tracked vehicle, designed for traveling over rough or soft terrain.) It seemed to be crying out, "Take me. I'm lonely." It was very tempting to just 'borrow' the bombardier - haul our gear to the river - then return it. No one would be the wiser. Or would they? After a quick consultation, it was decided; no harm - no foul.   To protect the innocent (which in this case, I'm not sure there was such an animal) I'll not mention which of us reached under the seat and found the keys. They were found, and it was all down hill from there.

Once you start in a life of crime, there seems to be no turning back! We glanced around to make sure no one was watching. We even looked skyward and didn't see anyone there either. Thirty minutes later everything was loaded in the boat and we were ready to return the bombardier...well almost ready. It hadn't gotten any cooler in the last half hour, and we were really getting a late start. Also, it occcurred to us that we just might be spotted returning the machine. We would appear as guilty as if we were just taking it. Funny we never thought of that before! It's strange when you're feeling a load of guilt that it seems someone is watching you. We were quite certain that someone was looking down on us and He didn't approve of this little caper. But, we rationalized that oilmen made big money and they got paid as much for walking as they did for riding.   We did park it where it could be seen from where it had originally been. We grabbed our oars and paddled off.   Let me explain here: at our tender age, our brains weren't fully developed yet. There has been some evidence that we were late bloomers in that department. I'm thinking of donating my brains to science because my wife has informed me that they are "one of a kind."

One thing we hadn't counted on, was how the river twisted and turned; then doubled back on itself. By ten p.m. we had arrived at Henry Halverson's little log cabin. Finding him absent, we went on in and tried to sleep on a couple rail bunks. We were very tired and really wanted to sleep, but the mice had other plans for us! There seemed to be hundreds of them and every time either of us dozed off, one or two of the miserable little creatures scampered across our faces. We soon forgot all about sleeping! After a nearly sleepless night, we were up and ready for nourishment - but certainly not here! There were a couple mice floating in the water bucket and little pebbles in nearly everything else. We went back to the boat and made coffee and hot cakes. Henry was a bachelor, and had a beautiful little place there by the river. It appeared though that he had been away for quite some time, because the mice had really taken over. In that back country it was expected that if no one was at home, a traveler could just go in and make themselves at home. The only expectation was that you refill the wood box and leave the place as clean as you found it.

Arne and I had a five gallon bucket, which we filled half full with sand. This was placed in the center of the boat. We made a fire in it and cooked as we went down river. That way we wouldn't be wasting any more time. It worked very well and there was no danger of the boat catching fire, due to all the water sloshing around our make-shift cookstove. Arne was so impressed with this little convenience that he suggested we patent it! In our exhausted state, we floated, ate and slept. We made toast when hungry or else endulged in our cache of raw turnips and carrots. I think we floated about fifteen hours that day. At dusk we heard the dreaded rapids ahead, so we pulled into the bank and made plans to camp.

Walking down river's edge to the head of the rapids, we looked them over and planned how we would run the first part of them. I glanced down at the ground near my feet and there lay an old Hamilton Railroad watch. Someone, perhaps years earlier, had been doing exactly what we were doing. The person probably pulled his watch out and accidently dropped it as he tried to put it back in his pocket. The hands were rusted to the face, but I pried them loose, wound the watch up, and it actually ran! I carried that watch for many years until I, too, lost it.

That night we built a big fire and went to sleep on the riverbank, with the sound of the rapids roaring away just beyond the bend. During the night, I dreamed that I was getting very hot. When I finally awoke, I realized my wool shirt was on fire! I leapt straight up and began beating and slapping my shirt to put the fire out. I caught a movement across the fire, and saw a black bear just rise up and fall over backwards. He high tailed it into the trees. Evidently, he had been watching us as we slept. When I jumped up, it had startled him enough that he fell over in his haste to escape these strange creatures who had invaded his space! Sleep was slow coming after that because, just as I would be dozing off, Arne would break out laughing, and I'd be wide awake again. The next morning, after a good breakfast of pancakes, coffee and wood ashes, we were reloading the boat. We looked up and saw a beautiful deer come down the bank to drink. She then walked into the water and swam across. The game in that wild country didn't seem to be afraid of us.

Up to this time we had been drifting along sedately, without too much excitement. Now the speed was really picking up. Even the mosquitoes were having trouble keeping up with us! I felt sorry for them, but life is not always kind. The rapids got increasingly worse the further we went, but we were able to navigate thus far. When our confidence had reached a sort of peak, it suddenly went from bad to worse to worser! Just ahead, a sandstone cliff seemed to rise up out of the water and turn into a great whirlpool, before somehow making its escape. The river rushed up to it and then fell away; making a gigantic rush into the next rapid.

Arne, in an effort to encourage me, hollered, **"Steve, this is where we meet our maker!"** Just about the time I thought things couldn't get any worse - they did! The force of the water pushed the boat up the cliff and pinned it there sideways! There we were, sitting perpendicular, looking straight down into the whirlpool and watching stuff being pulled under. At this point, I was thinking about that appointment with my Maker, and planning how I could explain to Him that it was all Arne's fault. I hadn't meant any harm. I was making a list of all my transgressions and realized there wouldn't be time. (List was too long!) Just then I felt the boat move a few inches. I glanced up and saw Arne standing on the topside with his oar wedged behind the boat. He was prying it away from the cliff an inch at a time. I joined in and eventually we pushed away. Our boat took a couple circles around the whirlpool before shooting out on the other side and downriver to more hair-raising rapids! They weren't as bad as this one had been.

All 'good' things eventually come to an end. We finally spotted the Smoky Bridge coming into vew. With the end in sight, our spirits lifted. We prepared to pull into shore just beyond the bridge. We could see some people standing on the bridge. They were yelling at us, but because of the noise of the rushing water, we couldn't understand what they were saying. We spotted a D8

Caterpillar stuck out in the center of the river. The top of its blade was sticking out of the water. The bridge had been designed to hold a certain limit in weight. This cat had exceeded that by quite a bit. So, the men had tried to ford the river. Because the water was so high, it had 'drowned out' just about midstream. What we didn't see, was a rope strung from the blade to the shore and then tied to a tree where the cat operator had been rescued. Arne screamed **"THERE' A RO......GLUG, GLUG"** as the rope caught the boat and flipped us into the river so fast, we didn't have time to be scared! When I finally resurfaced, I looked around for Arne. He was no where in sight. I figured he had met his Maker, as he had mentioned earlier! Suddenly he popped up like a cork, about twenty feet away! We then got down to some serious swimming - coats, boots and all! The boat, with all our gear was gone, so we tried for the nearest bank. The bank was getting further and further away. The river made a bend right there and it was pushing out. Arne yelled "We'd better try for the other bank!" We did - - and we made it! But we were now a mile downstream and on the opposite side of the river. There were still spots of snow laying in the shady spots under the trees. A cool breeze had come up as well. With our exhilerating swim in the icy water behind us, we began to shiver and shake. We were really, really cold! Stripped down to our birthday suits, we began to dance and cavort around to warm up; as our clothes hung in the trees to dry out.

About a week later, I met a man in town by the name of Henry Rice. He told me **"For a kid, you sure are a good swimmer!"** It turned out that he was one of those standing on the bridge, trying to warn us about the rope. I could only reply, **"When you're swimming for your life, you can can swim a lot better than you think you can!"**

By the time we were hiking out to the road and hitching a ride back to town, our parents had realized we were missing. One of the other Johnson boys had been compelled to tell them what we had done. Clarence Swanson, who later married my sister, Barbara, heard of it. He quickly assured my parents that "We had to be dead" He said, "No one could possibly make it through those rapids in this high water." They had arranged for the R.C.M.P to send out a crew to search for our bodies. Then - in typical Tom Sawyer fashion - we showed up!

Needless to say, there were a lot of mixed emotions. We were hugged for awhile and scolded for awhile. Eventually, we were questioned as to whether we had learned anything from our brush with death? We assured them we had; when actually we hadn't! There was no use telling them that. I did resolve not to let Arne talk me into anymore hair-brained schemes. Now, fifty years later, when asked if I had it to do over again, would I change anything? The answer is "NO. I wouldn't change a thing! Life is good!"

Jim Johnson - Steve Lusch - Arne Johnson

ALASKA OR BUST

Arthur Adolphson

I have always had an incurable disease known as "itchy feet." In layperson's terms, this means that I always had to know what was just around the corner and over the next hill. It was this disease that prompted Art Adolphson and me to plan a trip to Alaska. We were both seventeen and filled with optimism. As close friends, we had already shared quite a few adventures in school; and of course at that age, we figured we could handle anything the world could throw at us!

Our parents heard of our plans, and because they were hopelessly old fashioned, worried that we might get into trouble along the way! Years later, both of our parents had matured a lot. But at that time, we knew it was better not to tell them all our plans.

Art had a 1940 Ford pickup with a plywood canopy to carry all our supplies. These consisted basically of: Three barrels of gasoline, about three cases of pork and beans and couple cases of macaroni and cheese; and of course, our bed rolls. My mother had mixed up a large container of pancake mix, complete with a bottle of syrup. So, with these basics, we were well assured that we would avoid starvation. We also had a few tools to replace the clutch if necessary. It had been slipping pretty badly, but we didn't want to waste time to repair it before leaving.

It was early spring when we left (too early). The first day we drove until after dark and set our cots up alongside the road and in snow about ten inches deep! The smell of gas was too strong inside the canopy, forcing us to sleep outdoors. The next morning we realized that we had stopped right on the summit of

Steamboat Mountain. It was zero degrees Fahrenheit. It was too cold for picnicking, so we drove on to the foot of the mountain and ate cold beans from the can.

This was in 1954 when the Alaska Highway was still a twisting, serpentine trail. It was full of potholes, big enough to discourage all but the most hardy and foolish. We categorized ourselves with the former! One could still see parts of the road building equipment poking up through the surface. The army had given up on it and buried it, rather than bothering with repairs. The army, and unfortunate soldiers, who had to work on this road were ill prepared for the extremes in temperature and the ferocious mosquitoes that had to be dealt with in the far north. Most of them didn't have the foggiest idea what muskeg was, so a lot of machinery was lost or abandoned.

Temperatures in the summer were hot and muggy. It wasn't unusual to see the mercury drop to 20 and 50 below in the winter season. At this temperature, diesel fuel gels in the fuel tanks, causing equipment to stop running. Plus, none of the army trucks had heaters! By the time the road was completed, the war was over. It was then Canada took over the maintenance. Over the years it has improved to the point that today it is all paved. When Art and I went up this highway, conditions were still quite primitive.

We had planned on looking for jobs in Alaska. That was one reason we wasted little time going there. I have always regretted that we didn't take our time and explore more of the country and old mining settlements along the way. We drove until after dark; generally sleeping late the next morning. Our reason for this was that it was so cold in the mornings, we hated to crawl out of our warm sleeping bags.

One big hi-lite of the trip was at the Laird River crossing where there were a couple hot springs. They were still much in their natural state. The first spring was so hot it nearly took our skin off. The second one was just right. (Art definitely needed a bath by this time!) I couldn't really smell myself, but he was getting pretty ripe! This pool was about thirty feet across. A big tree had fallen across it, and was submerged about two feet under. It was just the right height to sit on and keep your head above water. We splashed and swam for two or three hours. (Much too long in that hot mineral water.) It was about six p.m. when we crawled out, and found that we were too weak and tired to travel further. We set up our cots and slept for twelve hours straight!

The following year, and for several years after that, Art and I drove trucks by there and we always tried to arrange a stop to soak in those pools. We stopped when it was minus 30 degrees, finding the snow melted back about five feet from the edge. We would undress on the edge, shivering and with teeth chattering. However, when we crawled out, we were so thoroughly heated through that we could afford to take our time dressing. It was seldom necessary to wear a bathing suit, because hardly anyone stopped at those hot springs in those days.

A couple years later, I had a terrible bout with boils - sometimes called carbuncles. They got so bad, I could barely sit or lie down. The doctors hadn't been able to help me and none of our home cures had worked either. At someone's suggestion, I caught a ride up there, and soaked in the mineral water for four days. I soaked until I was so weak I could barely crawl out. I then slid into my sleeping bag and slept like a dead man! Upon waking up, I got back into the pool for as long as I could stand it. On the second day, those boils starting lifting and by the fourth day, none were left. None of those thirty-odd boils even left a scar.

In Watson Lake, gasoline was selling for the astronomical sum of sixty eight cents per gallon! Today that sounds cheap, but then I thought it was so rediculously high that I took a picture of it. In Watson Lake someone had put up a sign of the mileage to their hometown. Other travelers had followed suit, until there were hundreds of signs. Watson Lake was an exciting place, with a lot of prospectors, speculators and quite a number of native Indian people...even a few tourists. I didn't realize at the time, all the interesting history we were passing along the way. We missed a lot of things that one can only read about now.

Eventually we drove into Whitehorse in the Yukon Territory, nearly dead from lack of sleep! (I don't know why we were in such a rush and drove such long hours.) We were both so groggy from driving, that we pulled into what we thought was a vacant lot. We just "crashed" inside the truck's cab. About twenty minutes later, we were jolted awake by someone banging on the cab. When we were able to pry our eyelids apart and rolled the window down, a very large and irate man was cursing at us. He said we were parking in their baseball diamond. He said, "Would you &@$*&%" tourists get this &%*# truck out of here and don't you be coming back!!" We meekly started the truck and drove away, so stunned that we didn't even try to argue (which was a wise decision on our part!) This event actually chased all thought of sleep from our heads. We went to a restaurant and drank coffee till it was good and dark; then drove about two miles out of town, set up our cots and went to bed.

I awoke to the sound of voices and lots of giggling. Peeking out from under the blankets, I discovered we were surrounded by a bunch of Indian kids. We had parked right on the edge of an Indian village - but this time, no one was mad at us! They (the kids) thought it was really funny and stood around jabbering in their own language, thus sparing us the knowledge of whether we were being insulted or not! Ignorance is bliss, I am told.

We spent the whole day wandering around Whitehorse; looking at the sights. There were about a dozen huge riverboats pulled up on the shore of the Yukon River. They were just fascinating. These were the old-time paddle wheelers and were finished inside with all types of exotic woodwork. The town wanted them removed and were offering them for sale for a mere dollar. The catch was that you had to move them out from there. I think they eventually had to burn some of them to get them cleared out. We also went out to view the famous "Miles Rapids," of gold rush days, where a lot of boats were smashed to bits by prospectors, driven to reach Dawson City and their dream of riches.

When we arrived at Canadian customs, they informed us that unless we had three hundred dollars in cash, the Americans would not let us enter Alaska. I could go, because I was an American citizen, but Art could not. This really put a damper on our spirits because, just like the Klondikers, we had dreams of striking it rich in Alaska. It took us at least ten minutes to get over our sorrow. When we learned that the U.S. Customs was thirty miles across the border, we decided to go that far so we could at least say we had been in Alaska. We celebrated by having pie and coffee at Scottie Creek; then turned around and headed for home.

One of the reasons we weren't completely heartbroken was because a friend, Melvin Reber, had offered us a job hauling dynamite, when and if, we came back. We wouldn't be able to get our chauffeurs license for another six months, but Melvin said he would cover for us so we could drive anyway. I think one of the reasons our parents hadn't argued too much about us going to Alaska was because they weren't exactly thrilled about us hauling explosives. If this were so, they were doomed for disappointment.

Just a short distance out of Whitehorse, a strange looking little man stepped out of the bush and flagged us down. He was

56

carrying a backpack that reached almost to the ground, and was about "bushed." I say "bushed", meaning tired. But he was more than tired. He had been alone, prospecting in the bush far too long. His gears had slipped a few cogs and he looked at us with suspicion, as if we might discover his cache of gold. His pack was so heavy, we could barely lift it. We eventually got it loaded in the truck and headed down the road. I was driving and I noticed he was really nervous. Art's old truck had cross-springs and loose spring shackles, so when you turned a corner, it leaned over pretty bad. I began pushing it pretty hard around the corners and he'd grip the dashboard with one hand and grab Art's knee with the other. By the time we pulled into Watson Lake, he was a wreck. He had told us he was going to eastern Canada to get away from the bush and prospecting.

However, about a month later, Art was hauling a load of explosives to Whitehorse and spotted him, hitching a ride north, again. I guess he'd been in the bush so long he couldn't stand civilization.

At any rate, we stopped in town. He grabbed his pack and disappeared into the crowd. It wasn't until years later that we learned we had actually picked up **"Yukon Joe."** He became quite famous and has even had a couple books written about him. It is said that when he was quite old, he buried two quart sealers full of gold somewhere west of Prince George. Unfortunately, he forgot where he put them!

Earlier, I mentioned a "crowd," because the place was swarming with people. At the time, we weren't aware of the fact that the Yukon and the Northwest Territories had just been admitted as territories of Canada. They had now been given the right to vote. Consequently, everyone within two hundred miles was in town. It seemed the influx was trying to drink Canada dry (that's a joke, so please laugh). The crowd was roaring drunk, so we pulled out of town to a rest area about five miles distant. We moved two picnic tables together, put our coleman stove and pancake mix between us and crawled into our sleeping bags on top the tables. It was a clear night and the stars seemed so close you could almost reach out and touch them.

About thirty minutes later, we bolted straight up in bed, awakened by the chilling chorus of timber wolves howling all around us. I'm sure there weren't as many as it sounded like, but there were enough to satisfy us! I have heard and seen many wolves since then, but have never experienced anything like that! It sounded like they were standing right outside our door -- except we didn't have the luxury of a door! I have heard people say that their "hair stood on end." Ours was standing at attention like it had starch in it! This went on for a half hour and as suddenly as it started, it stopped and all was deadly silent. We never heard them again, but I guarantee you it wasn't "out of sight - out of mind!" I figured if they came after us, I could out run Art, but it would have been my luck to trip and fall. Then, they'd get me instead! I'm glad they didn't get him, because a few years later, he married my little sister, MayJoy, and became my brother-in-law.

When the sun came up, all we had to do was reach over, pump up the stove and heat up the frying pan. The pancake mix was tossed in and we ate breakfast in bed.

That morning we drove back into Watson Lake to see if we could give the little prospector a ride, but somehow he managed to give us the slip. We did see a lot of "hung over" citizens though, and most of them looked pretty miserable. We had coffee with a young man who was extra miserable. He had awakened to find himself in bed with a lady who was a total stranger. The most frightening thing was the discovery of a wedding license with his and her signatures on it. Somehow, in their drunkenness, they had located a Justice of the Peace and gotten hitched! This could have only happened in the yet untamed Yukon! The fellow was quite shaken up and swore he would never drink again the rest of his life! The lady in question was still sleeping and he seemed reluctant to wake her up, so we never did get to meet her. I have always wished we had stayed around long enough to see how it ended, but we wished him luck and left Watson Lake for the Laird Hot Springs again!

Anxious to get home, we drove all that day and night. We never stopped until there was just the faint glow in the east where the sun would soon be making an appearance. We stopped on top of a hill and talked about what we wanted to do with our lives.

We decided to pool our money and count what was left. It came to $3.61. We still had plenty of pork and beans, but neither of us had any appetite for them or the macaroni and cheese! So we decided to splurge and have breakfast further down the road, at the first cafe we came to. A dollar went much further in 1954 than it does now.

We got out and pumped the gas tank full (enough to get us home) and still had over half a barrel left. I am not sure where the brain wave came from, but we did a very foolhardy thing. There was a big pothole right in the center of the road, so we emptied the rest of the gas into it, moved a safe distance back and tossed a match in it. After driving about a mile further, we stopped to look back and could see flames leaping about 10 feet high, still burning strong. There were several vehicles waiting for the fire to go out so they could get by. It looked as if they still had awhile to wait!

We stopped in Dawson Creek and blew our $3.61 for a good breakfast. In three hours we were home and eating our mothers good home cooking. We had left home with the motto, "Alaska or Bust" and had returned home "busted." However, in a week's time we were driving truck for a company called "Continental Explosives," later changed to "Explosives Ltd." We were as happy as if we had good sense!

BACHELOR'S CLUB

While suffering through the final year of school, my parents hinted that it was time for me to look for an occupation of some kind. The problem was that I wasn't sure what kind of work I should tie myself down to. I had worked in truck stops and various types of oil field work. I just couldn't stay at anything for very long.

I drove truck for Explosives Ltd. and did enjoy that, because it suited my sense of adventure pretty well. For a short time, I worked on oil rigs as well as seismograph (which is oil exploration). I enjoyed the latter because it took place mostly in wilderness areas. I found I was most content with anything that was connected to wild, unexplored country. As I approached the age of twenty, it seemed that something was missing in my life.

We had a fairly large group of friends around Valleyview. As a joke, we started what we called "The Bachelor's Club." I appointed myself President of this organization, but I soon realized that about all we had to discuss was the fairer sex! The unthinkable was happening all around me. My buddies were getting married one after the other! I finally came to realize that I might soon be president of a club of one! As might be expected, this finally dissolved all on its own.

I did have a homestead that I was trying to prove up, and I loved being out there. It was at the 'end of civilization,' with the nearest neighbor about five miles away. After a few days it seemed awfully lonesome. Dad owned the quarter section just west of me, but he was seldom there. It had a log cabin on it, so this is where I stayed when there. Of course there was no electricity, indoor plumbing or telephones. It takes a lot of money to prove up on a homestead. Money was something that was in short supply with me. Because of the situation there, I began spending winters driving truck for Explosives Ltd. It was interesting because we went all over the north country. I made quite a few trips to Whitehorse in the Yukon.

The law required two men to a truck when hauling dynamite, and my friend, Art Adolphson, and I managed to get paired up occasionally. There are some hot springs at mile 496 on the Alaska highway, and even if it was 30 below zero, we always managed to stop there for a swim. They were in their natural state in those days. In the winter we usually went in "au natural". The snow was melted back about five feet, so we would quickly strip off and jump in. We'd soak until we were heated as

60

much as we could stand. We would be so thoroughly warmed up that we could take our time getting dressed.

Another interesting trip I made was to Fort Simpson in the Northwest Territories. This is about three hundred miles down the McKenzie river from the Great Slave Lake. There was only a winter road which was basically just a bull-dozed trail made by the oil companies. The first time I went in there, we had to wait for nearly a week for the seismograph crews to arrive. At the time, Fort Simpson was nearly all natives, and there were only foot paths around the settlement. I spent my time exploring around town. What a delightful time it proved to be! The natives were very friendly and it was common to be invited in for tea. The influx of oil workers changed all that in the following years.

Years later I went there to live while managing an office for Ace Explosives. A small hotel/restaurant and the Hudson's Bay Trading Post were the only businesses at the time. The restaurant was like home. You ate what was served that day. There were no other choices. It was bitterly cold while I was there, so we had to keep the trucks running most of the time or they wouldn't start. This experience was the beginning of a love affair between myself and the north country. It still goes strong at the present time.

SOMEONE PLAYS CUPID
The Pastor of our church in Edmonton (Wendell Miller) told me that he was inviting his younger sister up. She lived in Oregon. Pastor Miller's wife, Beverly, began to make some strong hints that this girl was the one I would fall for when I met her. They began to push this pretty strong, so I decided I wasn't going to have anything to do with her when she arrived. Awhile later, they came to Valleyview for a church convention and brought her with them. I immediately began to regret my former decision, when I saw this very attractive girl, with long dark hair, climb out of the car. But, as I had made this 'boast' to some of my buddies, I felt obligated to carry it out for awhile. She (Wilma) had also been coached, so she was determined to ignore me as well.

Two weeks later there was a Youth Camp planned at Slyvan Lake. I heard she was going too, so I phoned and suggested that "since I had to come through Edmonton on my way, she could ride with me if she liked." She agreed, and although we didn't spend a lot of time together at the camp, I guess the seed was sown.

After camp I went to Wyoming to visit my sister, Barbara. Wilma rode back to her brother's place with some other guys from camp. I spent a couple weeks in Wyoming and it seemed I couldn't get this girl off my mind. Harvest was just around the corner so I headed home.

Of course I stopped in Edmonton to visit her. That was the straw that broke the camel's back! I recall her coming out to the kitchen where I was sitting. She was wearing blue jeans and a red and white striped shirt. She looked so good, I nearly choked on my coffee. That was the night that all my resistance went down the drain and I took the bait, hook, line and sinker!

The following day I went back to Valleyview and immediately went to work on the threshing crew. We started work at seven a.m. and quit at about six p.m. After work I would jump in my car and drive the two hundred miles to Edmonton. I'd get back home just in time to go to work again. As you can easily guess - this couldn't go on forever without something serious happening. Finally one night, just before starting back home, I explained that "If I wasn't so poor, I'd ask her to marry me." We had just stopped at a red light when I made this statement. The next thing I knew, she had her arms around me and informed me that she would marry me "even if we had to live in a cave!" About this time the cars behind us started blowing their horns. I realized that we had sat through the green light and the light had changed to red again! (About the color of my face.)

I do think that was the only time Wilma has ever lied to me. Since then I have suggested a couple times that living in a cave might not be a bad idea. She has refused both times! Since then, I have come to realize that you can never understand women. They'll say one thing and mean another! But how could we ever get along without them?

As soon as harvest was over, we went to Oregon so I could meet her family. Our plans were to get married the following Spring. So much for good intentions! Exactly thirty days from our first date, we tied the knot at her aunt's home in Pasco, Washington. It must have been a tight knot, because forty eight years later we're still in double harness and planning on another forty eight.

My Bride and I arrived back at Valleyview about a week later with no money, but lots of hope and plans for the future. I must admit that what I knew about women, and marriage in particular, could have been written on the back of a postage stamp - with room left over! However, being young and in love

62

can get you over some pretty big hurdles. Jobs were easy to come by, as the oil boom was on in Alberta. We moved into a ten by twenty foot skid shack with two rooms. (I, at least, thought it was great.)

I had been somewhat of a prankster at several of my buddy's weddings and they were set on revenge. Poor Wilma had to suffer for my transgressions, which apparently had been many! The first night home, our bed was upside down in the kitchen. When we got home from a reception held in Valleyview, the salt was in the sugar bowl and the sugar in the salt shaker. All kinds of shenanigans were played on us. The longest lasting was the limburger cheese that had been rubbed in the heater cores of my car. It smelled like something that had died until we turned the heater on. Then it was unbearable; certainly not a good thing in the middle of a northern Canadian winter! If we drove with the windows down, we could almost stand it! There were many times the temperature dropped to minus forty that winter. You guessed it! We never took any lengthy trips!

This car was a 1950 Chev and was still a pretty good car when I parked it behind the barn and abandoned it. As far as I know, it is still there - and probably still smells!

It seems like we just started having kids one after the other until we found out what was causing it. It's a good thing we did because our family tree is getting pretty big. In fact, a friend named Harry Rusk has started calling us a "Tribe!" I do have some regret that we didn't try for a world record though. I was willing, but Wilma said "absolutely, unequivocally, under no circumstance, never ever, **NO WAY**!" And that's putting it mildly. However, she sure does enjoy all the kids and grand kids. It would have been interesting to find out just how far we could have gone; but that's water under the bridge now.

I have always questioned whether I could have been more successful in life, had I taken things a little more seriously? I have thought about it occasionally and have decided I did the right thing in not letting success get in the way of all the fun and pleasure I have had by not being too serious.

Anyway, Wilma and I are both receiving old age pension now and life is pretty good. My main concern now is that the government doesn't go broke and spoil my pension. I plan on living to at least a hundred. The motive for this is primarily so I can embarrass my grand children some more, and use up all their inheritance!

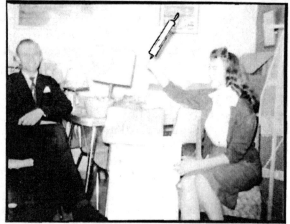

A COMBINATION OF HOMESTEADING,
MARRIAGE - MOSQUITOS AND WILDLIFE

I was young and foolish enough back then to believe that one could make a living on a homestead. Perhaps I should use the word optimistic, rather than foolish! I filed on 320 acres of bush land in the Peace River country. The terms were simple: Get 40 acres under cultivation on each quarter section; live on the place for six months out of the year, for five years. What could be simpler? A piece of cake! Right? If your answer is "yes," you're not any smarter than I was!

First you have to clear the trees off those forty acres (or eighty) in my case; you must plow the stumps out, along with the roots, put them into piles to dry and be burned; work this mess into a reasonably smooth field to be seeded. There! I put that all in one sentence, but it certainly takes much longer to do it! (At least two years and maybe three.) During this honeymoon period, there is a lot of outgo and absolutely no income. You have to find employment elsewhere to keep the wolf away from the door. That is IF you can afford a door! Some people (Animal Rights activists), like wolves, but I'm sure they've never had them at their door either!   I really don't want to go there, as I can get very passionate on the subject.

I was eighteen when I filed on my first half section. The process was slow proving up. Then, three months before I turned twenty three, I met this shapely brunette from Oregon. It was at this time, that I completely lost my senses.

I had only been twenty three for three days when I allowed her to convince me that I couldn't live without her. We tied the knot in Pasco, Washington. I painted a rosy picture of what a wonderful life we could have on the homestead -- and she fell for it. I may have neglected to mention how cold Peace River winters are. I purposely withheld information about the healthy mosquito population in the springtime. Another minor detail I overlooked mentioning was how muddy it could get when it rained -- which was whenever you didn't need it. One other item I may have neglected was to tell her how poor I was!

In those days the mosquitos were the terror of the entire population. Four of them could carry a 200 pound man right off the field and into the bush where they would kill him. I carried a rifle with me everywhere for protection. Well, all right... Perhaps I may have stretched it a little. It might take more than four!

Gradually, over time, Wilma and I became immune to those bloodthirsty varmints. Some people never did.

The Homesteader's Act provided a wonderful opportunity for many in Canada at the time. There was always plenty of work to be done, but it seemed we had more time for relaxation and fun then than the average family does today.

Hazards of Homesteading

Sandra in field of Grain stooks

Steve and Stephen

Stephen & Sandra with The Twins

MOOSE TAILS

So what if a moose doesn't have much of a tail? I needed a title to go along with some of my other stories. Alright? Besides that, Wilma encouraged me to share some of these true tales with you.

Because we never had any money to speak of, the advantage of having moose walking past our door was a blessing we really appreciated. My first attempt at moose hunting wasn't very profitable, but it was exciting. It was November and I was seventeen. I set out to bag a moose. I hadn't gone far when I spotted one about a hundred yards away. I was a good shot at targets, but on this occasion the sights seemed to be wobbling all over the place. I didn't realize it then, but I had contacted the dreaded disease known as "Buck Fever." I did hit him, but unfortunately, it was not fatal. He made tracks for parts unknown. There was a good foot of snow on the ground and it was snowing hard as I followed him at a fast trot. The moose was hit pretty hard and would lie down until he heard me coming. Then he'd muster up strength to start again. Had I been smart, I would have stopped and made a fire and rested awhile until he stiffened up. But I wasn't smart, and I followed him for about ten miles. By this time I had lost all sense of direction and it was getting dark. The snow was really piling up. I had to give up on him and I back-tracked until I had no tracks to follow. I was sincerely disappointed, not just because I failed to get my moose, but mainly because I had wounded a magnificent animal and had to leave him. I have a great deal of respect for all of God's creatures and I don't have much use for the so-called "trophy hunter." I really hate to see killing just for the sake of a trophy. On the other hand, many of the old timers would have gone hungry without wild meat. We used to can moose meat because we didn't have electricity. I still like to come in and heat up a jar of canned moose meat to eat with potatoes and any vegetable. It tastes great, and I believe it is far healthier than what the average family eats today.

One fall, during harvest, we had a couple of the crew sleeping on the floor in the front room. We only had two rooms at the time, and just a partital partition between them. When the dog barked, I looked out the window to see what was upsetting him. There were two moose standing in the yard. The men and I ran out in our shorts and I shot the biggest one, who was only about a hundred feet from our door. Poor Wilma wanted to come out and join in the excitement, but she had to cover her eyes with a blanket. I have a sneaking suspicion that she stole a peek anyway! When it was safe, she got up and cooked a great breakfast while we butchered the moose. What a great gift it was to have our winter's supply of moose meat. Yes, I did have a license and tag!

As a rule, the authorities were quite sensible men and sometimes 'looked the other way.' In my case, an example went like this: The local game warden drove into our yard one day when I was working on some broken down machinery. I invited him in for pie and coffee. As we walked onto the porch, I glanced down, and there in plain sight were four ruffed grouse. I had put them out of their misery earlier in the day, but hadn't taken time to clean them yet. I know he saw them, but he never said anything as we enjoyed our pie and visit. All the time, I was waiting for him to say something, and then as he was about to leave, he casually said, "You know, if I lived out here, I would never buy meat. But should you happen to shoot something out of season, it woudn't be wise to boast about it, because if someone reported you, I would have to investigate." With that he grinned and headed for his truck.

There were lots of grouse around. In the springtime they could be heard drumming all around the place. Our homestead was at the end of the road, and except for an oldtimer named Bill Goad, our nearest neighbor lived five miles away, closer to town. My Dad had homesteaded the land just west of us, but at that particular time, he was pastoring a church in town. Bill Goad still farmed with horses. He was a fine old gentleman and a great horseman. Bill treated his horses better than some people treat their kids. He had been born somewhere in the deep south (U.S.) and still had those southern manners.

We were really isolated in Fish Creek country and that's the way I liked it. About two or three months of the year, we had to park our car five miles away at Charley Gunn's place. From there we drove a tractor in because the roads were impassable.

Moose and deer were abundant, and black bear even more so. Bears were a real nuisance. They were so numerous and they loved grain, especially in the Fall before hibernation. One was allowed to shoot black bears all year around if they were on your own property.

*** ***

One time I did shoot a moose out of season. (Confession is good for the soul.) The proverbial wolf was at our front door and he hadn't brought lunch! Wilma and the kids and I were headed over to a neighbors one evening when a moose stepped up on the road in front of us. He pointed his long nose in our direction, scratched a line in the gravel with his toe and seemed to be saying by mental telepathy, "Too bad hunting season doesn't open for two weeks. I bet you don't even have your gun!" He snorted and I think that meant, "ha ha!" (He wasn't aware of the fact that I always carried a gun in my pickup.) It was impossible to ignore the challenge, so I dispatched him with a single shot to the head. The problem I now had was to get him off the road. The inconsiderate beast had dropped right in plain sight of anyone who happened along! I tore off to Dad's place, a half mile away, and got the tractor. I skidded him down behind the barn where Dad and I started the butchering process. But wait!! I could hear the game warden's pickup coming right up to Dad's front door! We washed up in the pond and headed for the house to face the music. I was feeling lower than a snake in a wagon rut. What a relief to see it was our friends, Arne and Merle Johnson. It's funny how, when you've broken a game law, all the trucks sound like the game warden's! Arne laughed at us, and then came down to help us with the butchering. He should laugh. He knew all about guilt. "Nuff said!" We ran the wolf away from our door and let him have the entrails.

Some of Arne's infractions bear repeating. The Johnson family lived by the Little Smoky river. They had come through the depression years by living on wild meat and a great garden; but old habits are hard to break. Arne could never resist shooting a deer or moose if they wandered too close to him. One day, he and my brother-in-law, Art, were driving on the Simonette road. They were in deep conversation about what beautiful animals deer were. They agreed it was a shame to kill such a beautiful creature. Art was congratulating himself on finally getting Arne to convert to his way of thinking. At this precise moment, a deer jumped out in front of them. Arne was out the door and had bagged the deer before the truck was even fully stopped! (That conversion hadn't lasted long!)

One day I made a a quick decision to go hunting. It was a perfect day. I drove down to Arne Johnson's homestead and found him working in the field with his brother, Sigurd. Sigurd was running the combine and Arne was hauling the grain to the granary. Harvest time can be very erratic this far north, so it is important to take the opportunity to harvest when you can. I told Arne I was going to look for a moose, but I could see he was too

70

busy to accompany me. Arne replied, "Not necessarily," and grabbed his gun from the grain truck and jumped in with me. Sigurd was understandably upset with this arrangement. When we got back, well after dark, the truck was heaped up way over the sideboards. Sigurd and the combine were long gone. The truck was so overloaded that the tires were almost flat. Arne had to crawl along home in first gear, or risk losing a lot of grain. To go hunting was a temptation that Arne could not resist. That's my kind'a guy!

*** ***

In time, we acquired a Border Collie that would jump into the back of the pickup everytime I started the motor. He was in the back when Dad and I were tooling along the road at about 50 miles an hour. Suddenly a moose boiled out of the brush along the road and ran across right in front of us. The dog barked and launched himself through the air at the moose. When he hit the ground, he rolled over five or six times and came up growling and barking like he was going to put moose on the menu! The object of his intentions had stopped and was standing, staring at us with a confused look on his face. The dog had lost his sense of direction and was barking in the opposite direction.

One time I shot a squirrel out of a tree in our front yard. As it fell to the ground, the dog was waiting to grab it. The only problem was that the squirrel wasn't dead! He clamped his sharp teeth into the dogs lip and hung on, as if his life depended on it -- which it did! The dog began squealing and shaking his head around until he dislodged the squirrel. From that day on, he hated squirrels with a passion!

This same dog had a constant war with coyotes and as soon as he spotted one, he was off like a shot. The coyote is a canny animal. It would get the dog chasing it, coyote's long tail just out of reach of the dog's jaws. The coyote would lure the dog across the field and into the treed area, where a couple more would be hiding, ready to gang up on him. He would come limping home, but he never learned his lesson. A few days later, after he had healed up, the process began all over again!

The collie would chase coyotes or squirrels, but he drew the line at bears. One time I had wounded a bear and it had run into a clump of willows. I knew it wasn't smart to go into the brush after a wounded bear, so I tried to sic the dog in to run him out. That dog just looked at me with a pained expression on his face. It was as if he was saying, "My mother didn't raise any foolish pups. You go after it yourself!" I tried bribery; then I threatened him with all sorts of dire consequences if he didn't obey me. The dog absolutely refused to budge. Finally I gave up and went in myself and fortunately I finished the bear off. After the dog was certain it was dead, he attacked it and acted like he was some great hero! That dog was just like some humans; they just don't appreciate how good they have it.

*** ***

My Dad loved the outdoors, and in the course of his 79 years, he has had many exciting adventures. Some of these were classed as "close calls." He was a 1st class marksman at both targets and live game. One thing he enjoyed was having us children throw coins and other objects into the air for him to aim at. The object of this was to see how many times he could hit the mark, before the object hit the ground. He seldom missed. As a young man in Cody, Wyoming, he was allowed only one turn at turkey shoots, because few people were willing to shoot against him.

Dad was in his mid-seventies when he set out walking east of my place, in search of a moose.It was right in the peak of the rut. We could hear the male moose grunting and calling to attract the cows. As most sportsmen know, it is during the rut that moose are extremely dangerous. One never knows how they might react to being fooled. Dad hadn't gone far when he spotted a large bull with an impressive set of antlers. It was only about a hundred yards off in an area that was thick with poplar and willow, making it hard for him to get a clear shot.

He had only taken three shells with him. He was carrying his 1895, 30/40 cal. Winchester. The moose began to move toward a bluff of thick spruce. Dad knew if he got into the trees, he wouldn't get another chance at him. He tried a shot through the shrubbery and missed. Jacking the second round into the chamber, he shot and connected. Instead of dropping, the massive animal turned and charged him! He was angry that some puny human had invaded his territory. The moose was approaching at terrific speed, with his head lowered. Dad scarcely had time to jack the final shell into the chamber. He did manage it though, and took careful aim right between the eyes. The moose was now about thirty feet away. Dad's aim was true and the impact drove the moose's nose into the ground. The huge animal skidded within a few feet of dad, who was feeling "a bit shaky." (His words.)

Dad had been bothered with arthritis for a number of years and was not as quick at getting around as he once was. I asked him what he would have done had he missed? He replied that his plan was to run and get behind a tree. I guess when you are about to be run over by a moose, your adrenaline rises and you can move faster than you think! I am sure that he really didn't have time to think. He was very proud of that moose!

*****

My family and I needed our winter's supply of meat. One frosty morning, I got up before breakfast. We had been married for ten years now, and Wilma had stopped giving me breakfast in bed. In fact, there were times that I even had to light the fire in the stove! I drove about 20 miles SE of Valleyview to an area where I knew there was a salt lick. Arriving just as it was getting light, sure enough I could see steam that betrayed the presence of a moose. It was just a short distance from where I had shut the motor off. I moved into position as quietly as possible and put a slug right behind his shoulder - trying for the heart. I heard the impact and knew I had him, so I just stood there and waited for him to fall. When I was sure it was safe, I moved in to cut his throat. Surprisingly, he was still standing. His legs were sprawled out and locked into position like an oversized saw horse. He was still alive, and I knew he couldn't last long. I hated to see him suffer, so I shot him the second time, with no obvious effect. He never moved, except to toss his head and glare at me. I waited as long as my nerves could stand, and then walked cautiously up to his head. He had actually died standing up and with his nose to the ground! I hit him right behind the front knee joint, and He slowly keeled over like he'd decided to take a nap.

When I was butchering that moose, I found he had been fighting. He had open sores all over his body and was badly fevered up. When I arrived home, we tried to cook some of the

73

meat, but it was inedible. Our St. Bernard wouldn't even eat it, and this was a dog who would eat practically anything! Wilma fed him all our table scraps, including coffee grounds, saurkraut, and ground wheat, but he turned his nose up at that moose meat! When Sampson wouldn't eat it, I knew I wasn't going to! I hated to see anything wasted, so I tried feeding it a quarter at a time to our pigs. (The ones in the chapter of The Great Pig Caper). The pigs thought it was delicious, but then they were always a few bricks short of a load.

I had wasted my moose tag, so we had to eat beef instead. We didn't like to butcher beef when it was our source of income.

*****

One time, our friend Arne was hauling a moose home. He had shot it near New Fish Creek. Wouldn't you know the game warden just happened along! He stopped Arne to check if all was legal. Can you imagine that! Finding all the paper work in order, he went back to check the tag attached to the antler. There was an audible snap as he popped it together and walked back towards his truck. The warden grinned and said, "You'd be surprised how many people fail to get those things snapped on right." Arne didn't blush often, but his face was red that time.

I should probably apologize to Arne for squealing on him, but I won't. If I did that, I'd have to do the same for other persons whom I plan to tell a few stories on. For that reason, I'll just have to leave it where it is. Arne can comfort himself with the fact that I at least thought about it, and "It's the thought that counts!" Right?

*****

The sun had just gone down when we all piled into our new car to go visit our friends, the Bradleys. I say "new car," in the sense that it was new to us. I had purchased a 1973 Pontiac Catalina just that morning. Wilma had been the one to drive it home, and now I wanted a chance to drive it too. I had no sooner turned the corner at the end of our driveway, when a moose, who seemed to be in an awful hurry, ran right over the top of the hood! All it did to him was cause him to stumble, but the car was a different story. The hood was of fiberglass, and it was completely shattered by the impact. The radiator was exposed and looking stark and naked! The moose just trotted away like he had something else on his mind. (Romance, perhaps.) We sat there in shock. This was an American made car, and I was never able to get replacement parts. We had to drive it like that for a year.

Then I traded it off. Moose simply have no respect for you! He was the only moose that I hoped would be eaten by wolves!

*** ***

I did see a moose killed by wolves once when I was selling drilling bits up in the Rainbow Lakes country. It was an extremely cold day when I saw a large moose run across the road ahead of me. Nine big timber wolves were chasing it. They hamstrung the moose right there. I had a front row seat to all the sickening action. The moose lay kicking and swinging its head while the wolves literally pulled it apart. They ripped its stomach open and had the intestines drug out while it was still struggling. I usually carried a rifle with me, but this time I didn't have it. I really regretted not having taken it!

The wolf lovers who re-introduced wolves back into Yellowstone Park, will tell you that wolves only kill the weak and sickly animals. (Not so.) That moose was a healthy adult in his prime. He was simply outnumbered by all those blood-thirsty wolves. Watching this made me sick to my stomach. I would hate to see all the wolf population killed off, but believe me, they were never an endangered species! There are plenty of wolves in northern Canada where few people live. It is an area as large as the lower 48 states. People, agriculture and wolves just do not mix!

*****

I am amazed at how quietly a moose with a 60 inch spread of antlers can move through thick brush. It is almost eerie how silently they ghost through the trees. My brother-in-law Jim, positioned himself at the base of a poplar tree and was calling with a birch bark horn. It was in the fall, near the extreme end of the rut. He called periodically with no response. He was about to go home, when he turned his head and discovered a big moose standing just behind him. Jim hadn't heard the moose, and it hadn't spotted him as yet. It was a toss up who was most surprised! As it turned out, the moose made its exit! Apparently he didn't think Jim made a good-looking partner!

As I mentioned, a bull moose in rut can be very unpredictable. It is better to get acquainted from a safe distance. I was about 16 years old when I learned how dangerous they really were. One Fall day, some friends and I were standing in front of the local garage. A wrecker, towing a little Willy's jeep, pulled in. The jeep was battered almost beyond description. The tow truck driver and the owner of the jeep got out and related what had happened. The owner had been driving along the old High Prairie road near the Little Smoky River, when he spotted a big bull moose. The moose was fighting mad and was thrashing the brush with his antlers. Intrigued, the driver got out of his jeep and began to take photographs of the action. It was then the moose saw him and charged. That fellow was too far from his jeep to escape, so he scrambled up a tree and out of reach. The moose wanted to do battle. He saw the jeep as an enemy and lowered his massive head and attacked it. He rolled the jeep over twice, plus punching dents and holes all over it. When he figured he had 'defeated the foe', he turned and wandered off towards the river. The man stayed up in the tree until the moose was out of sight. He then climbed down and caught a ride to town with the next vehicle that came along. He said that as far as he was concerned, the moose could have that country! He was never coming back!

*****

I feel that I was fortunate to grow up in a time and place where wildlife was abundant and there was room for everything. I was allowed the privilege to become acquainted with some genuine pioneers. They had a lot of worthwhile stories to tell to anyone who was willing to listen. I hope there is always a place to build a campfire and get away from the fast pace of the world around us. You know what? I'm starting to sound like an old man. I'm beginning to sound like my Dad. Come to think of it -- I'm glad!

THE END OF THE MOOSE TAILS

Photo by - Vonda Johnson

YET ANOTHER MOOSE TAIL

I can't resist telling a few more moose tails, so brace yourselves! I'm not sure of the exact dates, but it was while we were still living on the homestead. The Fish and Game Dept. decided to allow local hunters to apply for class 'B' Guide's license. Because of an over population of moose, they lowered the fees for non-residence alien hunters to fifty dollars. It was open for both cows and bulls.

I immediately saw a way to augument our income on the farm. Dollar signs began to dance in my head. Imagine making money at something you loved doing anyway! It would be like getting paid for romance, only not so stressful. Right? "Yes, you're wrong again!" First and foremost, I have never been able to charge a friend what it was actually worth; and suddenly I had a lot of friends! In fairness to these people, most of them left money hidden in strategic places where I would find it after they left. A downside to the hunting season is that it occurs at the same time harvest arrives on the scene. I could live with this, but my wife is a very practical, down to earth person and this often got me into trouble with her. For example, I might arrive home after dark from hunting and "Lambchops" would remind me of the eighty acres of oats laying out in the field waiting for a combine. I would reply that the weather forecaster predicted good weather for another week, and I was sure we'd get a moose tomorrow. It's absolutely amazing how quickly a week goes by when you're having fun. Besides, our radio was manufactured in Japan and what did they know about the weather in Canada! At any rate, I never got rich in the Guiding business.

At least once I lost a crop of grain because of an early snowfall. One time Wilma was complaining to a friend about me spending so much time hunting. Her friend replied, "Well, Steve doesn't drink, smoke or run around on you, so count your blessings!" I've always liked that lady.

One Fall, a friend named Raymond Noe came up. He brought his brother-in-law, Stan Tredwell and another friend for a moose hunt. (Raymond was from Washington and Stan from Oregon.) All of us had high hopes for a great hunt and the weather was just beautiful! We loaded the horses in my old Chevy truck and headed down to an area called Sweathouse Creek. As we pulled out of our yard it began to rain. It rained every day they were there!

In those days most of the roads were dirt and became nearly impassable when it rained. On a positive note, at least we didn't have to worry about the fact that my truck had no brakes. It was so muddy you couldn't go over twenty five miles an hour. If you took your foot off the accelerator, the truck would stop dead even without brakes.

We finally unloaded the horses and packed in a couple miles off the road where we set up camp. It drizzled rain every day after that. We never saw hide nor hair of a moose for two or three days, so we decided to move camp six miles south to a place where there was a natural salt lick. I was sure we'd eventually see some game there. We decided to hunt on the way down and return the next morning for the balance of our outfit. By this time we were all getting somewhat discouraged. As a result, Raymond and I took the horses and headed back to get the rest of our gear while the other two guys hunted around the salt lick.

Painting by Quita Crandall Pownal
(My 2nd cousin)

Due to the fact we hadn't seen anything for four days, we left our rifles at the old campsite. BIG MISTAKE!! About halfway back to the old camp we came to an opening about a hundred yards across. Guess what! Right! There stood a huge moose with antlers that would have made headlines! Raymond and I sat there and looked at it for ten minutes. I'm sure that thing knew we didn't have a gun. He just stood there and didn't even move when we whistled and hollered. Finally we rode away, with Raymond whimpering and whining, and with a stream of drool running out of the corner of his mouth! It was disgusting! The drooling, that is. We hoped that moose would still be there when we came back, but no such luck. He evidently had gone by our old camp and knew we had a gun this time. We simply had to chalk it up as a lesson learned! That was a once in a lifetime opportunity. I've heard it said that opportunity knocks but once.

The guys finally got two moose, but nothing could even come close to the one we let get away. We packed out after a week, with one tag unfilled. How nice it was to get home and dry out. We were starting to get web footed!

That night it quit raining. "Great!" you say? Not really, because it started snowing! Great heavy snowflakes bent the trees over until the smaller ones were almost touching the ground. A neighbor had walked over to visit. Later, when he started to leave to go home, Raymond offered him a ride in his jeep. A couple of us went along for the ride, leaving Stan home with Wilma.

We hadn't gone far before we found that the trail was blocked by trees which were weighted down with snow. One guy ran ahead, whacking the trees with a stick to dislodge the snow, allowing them to spring upright again.

We were on our way back home again when the jeep bogged down, so we were forced to walk the rest of the way in the dark. As we got close to the house we could hear Stan and Wilma talking. It was as clear as if we were standing next to them. I hadn't gotten wealthy enough to put glass in the windows, so there was just a piece of plastic stretched across the openings. Wilma was telling Stan about the wolves and coyotes that came up around the house and howled some nights. She told him how our kids liked to answer them and really get them going.

Now, Raymond is a great practical joker and was always playing pranks on people. Stan had been the recipient of many of them. Playing along with this opportunity just seemed the right thing to do! We let off a few drawn out howls and then stopped to listen. Stan says: "It sounds like they're right outside the window." Wilma (the expert) replied, "No. It just sounds like it, but they're probably quite a way off." We proceeded until we were almost under the windows and began to howl again. Wilma said, "My goodness! It sure does sound close. It sounds like timber wolves - not coyotes! I wish those guys would hurry and get back." Stan asked, "Aren't you worried about just having plastic over the windows?" Wilma said "I try not to think about it, and I don't want to talk about it. Maybe we should fire a gun out the door." At this suggestion we thought maybe we should go inside before someone got shot! We burst in, almost causing those inside to go into cardiac arrest! When things calmed down, we all had a good laugh over it. We sat around the wood stove and told a few tall tales.

I have known Raymond Noe since we were small children and we both lived in Cody, Wyoming. I was a few years his senior, so I had played a few pranks on him years ago. His Dad was our Pastor. I don't want to go into it at this point, but I will say that Raymond was a tough little kid! There was a faint possibility that I might be partly responsible for him getting in trouble a time or two.

Another time, a couple guys from Oregon, Carl and Glen Hatch, came up to hunt. We went southeast of my place to a big swampy area that had a lot of beaver ponds in it. This is prime moose habitat, but one had to plan on getting soaked a time or two crossing beaver runs and swamps. To make a long story short, these guys were good hunters and soon bagged a couple moose. Now was when the fun really started. The question was: "How do we get these moose out of the swamp to the truck?"

They had a good old four-wheel drive International, and Carl thought he could get pretty close to them. I warned them that this was not like Oregon, where there is rock under the soil. This country didn't have any bottom to it! I told them I'd have to go home and get my horse, Trixy. They could start the butchering while I was gone. After I left, they tried getting the truck over anyway. The truck was promptly bogged down so deep you could only see the top of the cab.

When I returned, they both looked pretty sheepish about it, but there was nothing we could do right then. We immediately went to work trying to get the moose out to the road. I had a good heavy stock saddle on Trixy and my idea had been to quarter the moose and tie two quarters together and hang them over the saddle. I'd have to make five trips out of it. However, it was hot and humid and I thought I'd see if Trixy could skid them out a few yards at a time. I tied a heavy nylon rope around the antlers and the other end to the saddle horn. I picked up the halter shank and headed out of the swamp.

When Trixy felt the weight of the moose behind her, she really dug in, and I had to run to keep ahead of her. Somehow I managed to maneuver around a beaver run, but Trixy had so much momentum going, she knocked me down in the run! She plowed straight on through! The run was about five feet deep, and I went right to the bottom. I came up just in time for the moose to slide over me; pushing me under again. I felt like I had swallowed five gallons of swamp water, but it probably was only one! When I finally got up and got my eyes cleared, the horse and moose were a hundred feet away and going strong! When we finally caught up to Trixy, she had stopped by the road - her sides just heaving. Aside from the near drowning, this had worked so well that we went back and tied her to the second moose. I slapped her on the rump and got out of the way! She got this one out all by herself and was waiting for us when we arrived.

It was late by the time we got the moose butchered, but Carl and Glen were worried about leaving their truck back there over night. We went to my Bro-in-law's place to see if he might have any brain waves as to how to get it out. It just so happened that the Church convention had just ended and when we arrived, there was quite a crowd of people at Art's place. One was the Overseer of Western Canada, Hugh Edwards. He was all dressed up in a suit and tie. He asked if he might ride along with us. I tried to discourage him because I knew it was going to be a dirty job, but he insisted. With Art's big grain truck and a couple hundred feet of cable, we were on our way. There were more of us now and we piled into a couple vehicles.

After much struggling, we did get the truck out, but not before the Overseer fell into the bog! He was covered with mud from head to toe! I was feeling real bad about him ruining his suit and all, but he was a great sport. He later told me that he hadn't had so much fun since he was a little kid.

Carl and Glen headed back to the States with their moose. The next year they returned with their parents. We have been good friends over the years. Carl died of cancer several years ago in Salem, Oregon. The family asked me to officiate at his funeral. We had been planning an Elk Hunt shortly before he learned he had cancer. I had moved to Oregon about one year previous to this; and had to say goodbye to a good friend.

To lighten the mood a little, I'll have to tell you of another fellow who came up to hunt. Pete Chappel has been know to boast about some good shooting on occasion. When I heard him tell this story on himself, it was just too good to keep quiet.

Pete had acquired an expensive hunting dog that he was training for bear hunting. He was on the trail of a bear when a deer dashed across the trail. The dog took off after the deer! Pete called to him to return, but his instructions were ignored. Pete aimed over the dogs head with his 7mm magnum and touched one off. The idea was that the bullet passing over the dog's head would make a loud popping sound, from the air being displaced by the bullet. He thought this would get the dog's attention. It worked - up to a point! It did get his attention all right, but not the way Pete intended. Either the dog jumped over a stick or something - or else Pete's aim was off. He blew the dog's brains out. However, to leave this on a more positive note: The dog has never chased a deer since, unless there is a dog heaven. We hope so, anyway.

THE GREAT PIG CAPER

It all started with my good friend, Jock, giving me a pig in payment for some work I had done. What I wasn't aware of at the time, was that this female pig was pregnant. She was thin, so I began feeding her grain and other good stuff to fatten her up. Pictures of bacon, ham and pork chops were dancing in my mind, and at times I found myself drooling over what was soon to be. She seemed to be fattening up much faster than I expected, but I went blissfully ahead, ignorant of what was to happen.

One day a short time later, our children had left for the road to catch the school bus. They came rushing back to the house saying, "Daddy come quick! Something is wrong with Gertrude!" Wilma and I went running, thinking a coyote or some other predator was starting Thanksgiving a little early. All four kids were streaming out behind us. A quick glance revealed the truth. Gertrude had given birth to ten miniatures of herself. She didn't seem to appreciate our interest in her extracurricular activities. Needless to say, the kids had missed the school bus, which meant a thirty mile trip to town. Already the pig was causing me headaches. Well, butchering was delayed somewhat, but now we would have ten times as many pork chops. At least that was the plan, until the kids began making pets of them. They didn't exactly like the idea of turning the piglets into bacon.

It didn't take long before the pen, which had been plenty roomy, became overcrowded. Not only that, but feeding them all was beginning to be a lot of work. They ate like pigs (pardon the pun!) Also the grain supply was going down fast. Just a short distance away I had planted five acres of red clover, which was about two feet high. Beings I was never one to exert myself (if there was an easier way) it didn't take me long to take one section of the pen down so they could fend for themselves. After all that, for some reason the pigs didn't want to leave the familiarity of their pen. I had to drag them squealing from the pen, and giving them a swift kick to encourage them to head for the clover. That was the end of them being pets, or even tame. They soon became as wild as deer and just as leery of anything standing upright!

We owned a huge St. Bernard named Jed, who was a wonderful pet and great guardian of our children. For a reason we were unable to figure out, the piglets formed an uncommon attachment to Jed and began to follow him around as though he was their mother. Instead of being insulted, Jed seemed quite proud of this accomplishment. We began to see him leading the pigs all over the place. I didn't think it showed much intelligence on his part, but the family thought it was kinda funny. He wasn't too picky about the company he kept.

One fine Tuesday morning I headed for town to our local livestock auction. I ended up buying thirteen head of Hereford feeder cattle to add to our herd of Angus and shorthorn cows. I owned an old Dodge one ton. They were packed in so tightly there wasn't room for them to move. In fact, I asked them to hold their breath until I got the end gate closed. Of course they did that for me! During the course of the day, the weather had turned ugly. It was beginning to rain, as I headed home. I was rather proud of this load of calves and wanted to show them to my Dad who lived a half mile from us. Arriving at my parents place, I saw their lights were out. As I backed up to leave, the truck gave a little jerk.

What I didn't realize, was that the 'jerk' had knocked the end gate loose and the calves began to drop out one by one. When I got home and backed up to the loading chute, I only had one left. That calf took one quick look at me and leapt over the side, disappearing into the darkness. (Wilma said there were a couple times she wished "she had taken a quick look and run off herself!" But it was too late after she realized what she had gotten herself into.) To make matters worse, the calves were strangers, and there were no fences for thirty miles. It was now darker than the inside of a cow! To make matters worse, it was beginning to snow like it had no intention of stopping! I drove back down the road to Dad's place, but couldn't find a trace of the bunch. So I did the only thing I could. I went home and crawled into bed, thinking it couldn't possibly get any worse.

The next morning, before it was even light enough to see, I had my faithful horse, Trixy, saddled and ready to go. By now there was 8 inches of new snow on the ground. Trixy was looking at me with that look that said, "Why me? Why is it always me?" So I reminded her that she was the only horse I had at the time, and that unless she smartened up and earned her keep, I might sell her to the glue factory. (Her attitude didn't seem to change much.)   The one thing in my favor was the new snow, as any tracks would be fresh. I caught up with the first three runaways about 6 miles north of home, and brought them back to be with the ones I already had. Then I went looking for the rest. I found them in little bunches as far as 10 miles away. All the way home, they acted like I was taking them the wrong direction.   I talked real sweet to them, and finally accounted for all thirteen.   Now I could finally relax!

It was then that Wilma came and informed me that Mr. Jensen had phoned, saying that there was a St. Bernard in his yard, with ten pigs following him. Jensen's place was two miles away. It was getting late and poor old Trixy's attitude had gone downhill. My own sweet disposition was beginning to sour on me, but I had no choice but to head for Jensen's. I failed to thank Wilma for that information, because my backside felt like it had been driven through the frontside! On arriving at the Jensen farm, I painfully slid off my horse and grabbed a chunk of firewood, which I forcefully threw at Jed. I told him very kindly, but clearly what I thought of a dog who was ignorant enough to associate with pigs! He didn't hang around to hear all my thoughts, but headed for home like his tail was on fire! The meanest thing he did though, was to leave his ten little friends behind for me to round up! It was like a rat abandoning a burning ship. Somehow nobody ever told me that you can't drive pigs - especially when you are already mad at them. They seemed to have picked up on that fact with no training.

I prefer not to go into detail on the rest of this little caper, but I will pass on a little handy advice here. If you are ever trying to move a herd of pigs from point A to point B, don't go galloping ahead into the bunch barking what you really think of them and their mother! It tends to hurt their feeling and makes them real hard to control. In fact, this particular group scattered all over the place and simply refused to be herded. I ended up taking one or two at a time and steering them in the right direction; then going back for a couple more, until I could see the lights of home shining through the trees. I then abandoned them, and made tracks for the kitchen table. The next day, they were all in the yard following that stupid dog.

When the snow got deep, and those pigs started rooting up the lawn at night; then coming up to sleep on the porch, it was just too much of an insult. I secretly made plans for their immediate future, which I will relate to you in another chapter.

ALMOST THE END.

PIGS --FINAL EPISODE

Life on our little ranch in the Peace River country fell back into a somewhat normal routine after our escapade with the pigs and the dog. The pigs still followed Jed around. He still thought he was king of the hill, and we finally got the cows sorted out and in their proper pens and feedlots.

The main "fly in the ointment" was that herd of unruly pigs. The snow was now two to three feet deep, and the temperature holding in the below zero range. The pigs were so wild we couldn't get within 200 yards of them without them raising their curly tails and dashing for the timber. An idea began to formulate in my devious little mind as how to bring about their capture. It was further driven by the eventual aroma of bacon frying. I tried shooting them, but that only netted me one porker, while the rest left in nine different directions and stayed there until dark. I realized this method would take a lot of time and patience, of which I was running short! The ornery things were actually doing very well for themselves, and staying fat. But this came at the expense of our beautiful lawn grass and my sweet disposition. They sneaked in at night while we were sleeping and methodically rooted up the grass underneath the snow. As a further dare and insult, they crept onto the porch and slept there by Jed. They were always gone before daylight, but not without leaving their calling cards. Wilma took a rather dim view of this discourtesy. She seemed to live with the constant fear that the preacher would show up and find pig droppings on the porch.

Wilma's fear came to pass, except it was with a newborn calf..and not the pigs. Very early one bitterly cold morning (four a.m. to be exact), while making my rounds checking the cows, I found a cow had just given birth. I knew the only sensible thing to do at twenty below, was to bring the baby to the house to dry out. I fixed a secure little nest for it in Sandra's corner of the bedroom -- or at least I thought it was secure.

Later that morning, I was down at my parent's place when the phone rang. It was my sweetheart telling me that the calf (which I had forgotten to tell her about) was slipping and sliding around the kitchen. The reason it was sliding, was because it had made a 'boo boo' and was spreading it all over the floor. Wilma was most unhappy and asked me who else was at Mom and Dad's? I told her it was the preacher. She gave me strict orders not to let him know why she had called. But she ordered me, in no uncertain terms, to excuse myself and hurry home to help take care of the mess! The kids were home, because it was Saturday. They were having a great time with the calf and thought the whole incident was hilarious. There seemed to be a lot of excitement going on in our "home on the range!"

It so happened that the preacher had been raised on a farm. I figured he would understand, so I let the secret out. We drove to the house together just In case I needed an extra cowhand! Wilma finally forgave me, but only after I reminded her that the Bible said we must "forgive if we are to be forgiven." Also that the Lord knew all about her wicked thoughts that day.

Now, back to the pigs! We had to do something soon, or there would be no lawn left. Wilma had already broken the handle off one of her kitchen pans by cracking one of them over the head. She caught that pig, and the others, sleeping on the porch with the dog again. Any good cowboy knows how to trap critters when the need arises, and I continued with plans for their demise. I built a plywood pen and made a gate that I could close with a hundred foot rope from inside the kid's bedroom. Then I spread a trail of rolled oats leading into this ingenious contraption. The porkers followed the trail of goodies right into the pen. I gave a mighty pull on the rope and the gate slammed shut. The key word here is "slammed." At the sound of the gate closing behind them, all nine, in perfect unison, and with the agility of deer, leapt over the sides and into the woods! There was a need for some major improvements to this remote controlled devise! This time, I built the pen eight feet high and made another trail of rolled oats. The pigs never showed up for about a week. Then, like the bunch of thieves they were, they started coming in at night. I kept the trail of oats out there, and finally their greed overcame their good sense. We saw them sneaking in, one at a time into the big pile of grain in the back of the pen. I yanked the rope; the gate slammed shut and they were finally trapped! There was a lot of commotion in the pen for awhile, but the trap had worked!

The next step was to haul the sweet little things to Grande Prairie to the packing plant, and have them butchered. I phoned and bribed my good friend, Terry Johnson, with lots of free pork if he would haul them in with his pickup. He came right out, and with a little luck and lots of sweat, blood and tears, we got them loaded and Terry headed for Grande Prairie. I didn't go with him, so I missed the final event of the wild hog caper. The trip had gone well, and Terry was feeling light and carefree. It had been an easy trip thus far. He backed into the loading chute and called the attendant over to unload. Terry was anxious to get this done, so he could go have coffee in the city. (Terry always had coffee before going somewhere - when he arrived and anywhere inbetween!) The attendant climbed up, looked in and bellered, "Open the gate!" There was no need to open the gate! The pigs were gone over the edge as though it was only 4 feet high. They quickly scattered up and down the railroad tracks. It looked like Terry might have to delay his coffee break for just a short while. The attendant quickly recruited everyone who worked in the place, including the receptionist and typist. He nabbed every able bodied person in sight. The pigs were so confused they didn't know what to do. (There was no field or timber to hide in.) Finally the recruited workers managed to get them rounded up and penned for good. (And Terry went for his well deserved coffee break!)

So the curtain comes down on the most frustrating pig operation of all times! I swore off raising pigs for the rest of my life, and I almost kept that promise. I did have one lapse of good judgment some years later, and it was no more successful than my first one. Perhaps I'll tell you about it another time. I think I will get Wilma to fry me up a little feed of BACON. That will be <u>my revenge</u>!

BEAR TAILS

Note: I would like to dedicate this chapter to two young boys named Coleman and Chad and to their sister, Michelle. These three listened to their Grandpa tell some real "windys" about some close escapes he allegedly had with bears in the old days. Chad listened with his mouth wide open, because if Grandpa said it, it must be true! Coleman, who is somewhat of a scientist, was skeptical and kept interrupting. The stories seemed a bit too far fetched for his logical mind. Michelle just sat and smiled. She accepted them as good stories, but was too sophisticated to let me believe she was fooled. Well Kids, I love you all for what you are and who you are. I want you to know that what you are about to read is all the truth. I promise!

There were a lot of bears living around our homestead in New Fish Creek. They were either a source of amusement or one of annoyance. My first experience at shooting one was when I was sixteen. My Dad had bought a quarter section of land from Pete Pederson. Pete's wife had just passed away and he wanted to move away.

Just west of us lived a fine old bachelor named Bill Goad. Bill still farmed with horses and had just cut a good crop of oats. The bears were packing the bundles into the woods and eating them. Bears love oats, especially in the fall before hibernation. There was one big, old bear that would walk out in the field; put a bundle under each arm; stand up and waddle off the field just like a man might do. Bill had lost way too many oats for his liking, but he didn't even own a gun. He came by and asked if I would come over and try to do away with this bear that was eating up his profits. Davy Crocket had killed 'a bar' when he was only three, but I had never killed one. I was anxious to change that pattern as soon as possible.

I could easily see where the bear had been coming out of the woods, so I staked out a spot down wind from it. It was late afternoon and I sat and waited for him to come out. I didn't have to wait long before he poked his snout out of the bush and cautiously looked around. When he decided there was no danger, he walked out in the field. He picked up a bundle under each arm and turned to walk off to have a picnic in secret. He made a big target, and my sights seemed to be wobbling a lot. Finally I centered it where I thought his heart would be and pulled the trigger. He let out a plaintive wail, dropped the bundles and

90

Streaked the thirty yards to the trees where he disappeared from sight.

Bill's house was about two hundred yards away. He yelled, **"Did you get him? Did you get him?"** as he came running out to where I stood. I was sure I had hit the bear, but he had gone into the trees at pretty good clip. I wasn't sure how bad off he was. The excitement was intense and I was shaking a little. But I didn't want Bill to know what a greenhorn I was. I led him over towards the place the bear had disappeared and was ready to shoot again, should he charge me. Bill was hanging back quite a distance and I realized he was as scared as I was. That didn't make me feel any more secure!

I cautiously pushed a willow bush out of the way. There was this big, black monster with jaws wide open and ready to charge! I emptied the next five shells from my 30/06 into him, but he never even moved. This was the moment I realized I had just murdered a burnt stump! It sure wasn't about to go anywhere with five bullets buried in it! Bill was all excited then and hollered, **"Is he dead?"** I hated to admit what had just happened, but the evidence was right in plain sight. By this time, Bill was peeking over my shoulder; poised to run if anything moved. Nothing moved! The stump was still anchored to the ground. Between gusts of laughter, Bill admitted it did look a lot like a bear to him too.

I was disgusted with myself and sliding a few more shells in into the rifle, I stepped around the stump. There – not ten feet away lay a very dead bear! I turned around to inform Bill, but it was no use. He was laughing so hard, he wouldn't have heard me anyway. When he could finally talk again, he said, **"By ginger, Steve! You shore slaughtered that old stump! It ain't goin' nowhere."** When I showed him the dead bear, he sure was happy. As far as I know, he never told anyone about the stump with all the lead in it. Over the years I have bagged a lot of black bears, but none can compare to that one for sheer excitement.

In those days we all had wooden granaries that were made of shiplap lumber and usually held about a thousand bushels. The bears would come in at night and pry the bottom boards off with their powerful forearms. They spilled a lot of grain out on the ground, which was a chore to clean up. It was also costly. We invented all kinds of schemes to stop them. Most were fatal to the bears.

We had a granary located beside the barn where we stored grain for the livestock when we had them locked in the corral or barn. Bears have a very keen sense of smell, and it didn't take long for them to sniff this feast out. We tried setting traps and many

91

other gimmicks to stop a certain bear that kept coming. Some nights, my friend Arne and I would sit on top of the barn, hoping to spot the culprit coming in. We stayed until we got so cold we'd go to the house for some hot coffee. Then we'd hurry back, only to find the bear had been there, spilled the grain and run off as soon as he heard us coming back. Next we left the door open so he wouldn't have to rip the boards loose. We wired a double barrel, ten gauge shotgun to the doorway so he would trigger the thing when he entered, and hopefully shoot himself. All that was accomplished was a big hole in the opposite wall where the buckshot went through! I don't know how he avoided that, but he kept coming back. Now he was ripping bags of clover open that we had stored inside! This bear was too smart for his own good.

In desperation, we got some strychnine pills and mixed them up in a quart of honey. We poured this deadly concoction into a gallon can and placed it in the doorway. The next morning we found that the bear had licked up all the honey but the pills were left rattling around the bottom of the can! The more he outsmarted us, the more we were determined to stop him.

Finally we settled on the idea of wiring a rifle about ten feet up in a big poplar tree. We hung a small bag of honey from the trigger. That way, when he grabbed the bag of honey in his teeth, he'd shoot himself. We figured he would be hanging onto the tree with his claws so he'd have to grab the bag with his mouth. We heard the gun go off in the night. The next morning there was a pool of blood at the base of tree; but no bear. He never came back, so he must have crawled off into the bush to die. My stupid dog again flatly refused to go in after him. We had to be satisfied with the fact that we had outsmarted him; at least for that year!

I went to work for Century Geophysical, a seismograph crew, one summer. The crew consisted of about thirty men. I was on the survey crew. In those days, they had a garbage pit about thirty yards from the cook shack. The bears would swarm there at night to feast on the refuse. They threw away more good food in one day than most families eat in a month. It was a real bonanza for the bears and a few foxes. The problem there was that the cook and his helper had to walk past there at four every morning to get breakfast started. The bears had gotten so bold they would hardly move over to let them by. This annoyed the cook so much that he got a twelve-gauge shotgun and loaded it with rock salt. His opportunity came the very next morning when a bear walked by the kitchen door and stopped to peer inside.

This was too much for Ray LaCroix, the cook. He snatched

up the gun and just as the bear turned to run, Ray shot him in the rump with both barrels! The problem this presented was that the bear just happened to be facing the Survey shack. He continued at a speed that would have made a race horse green with envy! The Surveyor, Leo Quinian, had just come out the door rubbing the sleep out of his eyes, when he was bowled over by Mr. Bruin! He hadn't even seen him coming! I occupied the top bunk just inside the door. I was rudely jolted awake by Leo. He burst through the door and landed on the pit of my stomach! He was stammering something about a bear attacking him! I had been sleeping soundly until then, but I got up and looked out to see what all the excitement was about. However, everything seemed peaceful out there, so I thought he had been dreaming. The only thing I heard was the cook and his helper roaring with laughter. I figured Ray must have told his helper an extremely funny joke. The truth came out at breakfast that morning. There was a lot of good natured teasing at Leo's expense.

It was against the law to kill bears in the garbage pits because it was considered baiting. This bear had a sore bottom for a few days, but it didn't keep him away for long.

My friend, Bud Hardman, was on an oil crew up by Rainbow Lakes. They had the same problems there, with bears coming in and scaring the workers. One huge black bear was an especially bold pest. They determined to try to teach him better manners.

A sheet of metal was laid on the ground and wired to a tasty chunk of meat that was hung about six feet above it. The men then wired it to 110 volts of electricity; fastening the ground wire to the metal sheet. Sure enough, as his habit had been, Mr. Bear came padding in just before dark. A smaller bear was following at his heels. The large bear immediately smelled the meat; walked out in the center of the metal sheet; stood on his hind legs and clamped his teeth into the meat. The results were even better than the guys had expected! His four legs shot out at right angles to his body, causing him to flop over on his back. He leaped up and hit the smaller bear with a blow that knocked him end over end! The little bear took off for the tall timber. He was squalling like his life was in extreme danger - which it was! The big bear shook his head, not quite understanding what just transpired. He cautiously stood up and tried for another bite with similar results! This time, he got back on his feet and walked off, looking over his shoulder and growling at an enemy he could not see. He probably went to bed hungry, and with a sore mouth that night! This had worked so well that the guys left the apparatus in

Place. After that, every bear that came around was greeted with a jolt of electricity. In time they began making wide detours around the camp to avoid the cruel welcoming committee.

Before Wilma and I acquired livestock, we spent the winters in town because the roads were so treacherous. As soon as Spring allowed we'd move back to our little log cabin on the homestead. One Fall, I had stored some wheat in the cabin. On our first day out, I moved the grain out and Wilma cleaned up the place. She had it looking nice and cozy by nightfall.

Sandra was three at the time and Stephen about two. As Wilma was getting them ready for bed, she looked out the window. She spotted two bears coming through the garden plot and heading straight for the cabin. It was obvious they had been coming inside and helping themselves to wheat while we were living in town. Wilma called me to the window and we held Sandra up so she could see them too. I grabbed my rifle and stepped out the door to greet them. By now they had split up and were walking to opposite corners of the cabin. I shot one and then turned to get the other as he was retreating. He dragged himself a short distance into the trees and died there. After hearing the shots, Wilma went ahead and got the kids settled for the night.

I hung the bears up on the cat blade and skinned them out. That is how Sandra saw them the next morning when she awoke. They were hanging there with their hides off, naked as Jay birds. That picture remained in her mind.

Later that summer after the crops were in, we drove down to Oregon to visit Wilma's folks. Grandpa Miller was in the back yard talking to Sandra. He came in the house laughing and said that Sandra had been telling him bear stories that were a little far fetched. In his deep Missouri accent, he said, **"Sandra told me, 'My Daddy just shoots the 'hyar' right off them 'bars'!"** We realized then that the last time she had seen them, the bears were alive and had their hair on. Soon after that she had heard the gun shots. The next morning when she saw them, they were hanging naked on the cat blade. *(Sandra must have inherited her story telling abilities from the Millers, because she got pretty good at it!)*

Wilma's parents owned a country grocery store outside Stayton, Oregon. One day Sandra followed her Grandpa into the store and then filched some candy. She was headed out with it hidden behind her back. Sandra thought it was hidden, but Grandma Miller could easily see it as she went by. Grandma took Sandra to the side and told her very gently that if she wanted candy all she needed to do was ask. She would gladly give her some, but it was wrong to steal it. Sandra looked up at her so seriously and said, **"I came down here from Canada to see what kind of a woman you are, and now that I know, I'm gonna go back home!"**

The bear stories are endless. There were so many bears wandering around in those early years. Perhaps I can share more stories at a later date.

MORE BEARS

They say ignorance is bliss and that is the only excuse I have to offer for the way I treated my beautiful bride. Wilma had spent most of her life where the roads were paved, and where there were no bears. On the other hand, I had been nurtured on tales of mountain men and hunting stories.

By the time we were married, I had almost become immune to having bears wander through the front yard and peeking in the windows. This had to be terribly frightening to Wilma when she first arrived in our little patch of paradise. She tried to be brave and not let her 'wild man' know how scared she was.

One nice day I was headed to the field to disc up some new breaking. Wilma decided to load the two little ones in the pickup and drive to Valleyview to do some shopping and to visit a friend, Hulda Perron. It was a distance of twenty miles. She was following the ruts out to the highway and had gone about three miles when the truck jumped the ruts. They ended up in the ditch, with the truck high centered. She knew I didn't expect her back until evening, and it would be a long wait before I'd come looking for her. We had no phones, so her only option was to start walking and hope the bears didn't get her and the kids. She didn't realize that if you make enough noise, a bear will take a wide detour in order to avoid you. Also, if one did come to look, it was usually just curious and generally would run away if you yelled at it. There is the slight possibility that I had 'fed her fears' a little, so I could impress upon her how brave I was! It was kinda nice the way she would cuddle up to me after I had run some big bad bear off 'just to protect her.' A man has to use every advantage possible to counter a woman's (supposedly) superior intelligence.

With her heart in her throat, she picked both children up and headed through the trees. She whispered to them that they should be very quiet so the bears wouldn't find them. I spotted them coming across the field, and drove the tractor over, wondering what the problem was. I shut the motor off, and there's a slight possibility I may have sounded angry when I asked, **"Well, what's wrong this time?"** Wilma has these big brown eyes that can look so innocent and hurt. They can make me feel guilty, even when I'm not. When she looked up at me, with the water works about to flow, I knew I had to pull some sweet talking out of my bag of tricks. (I didn't want to be sleeping on the back porch!) Well, that may be stretching it, because at the time, we had neither back or front porch! I did my best, and it seemed to work that time.

Black bears were very common in our neighborhood because of the abundance of wild berries. We had to compete with the bears if we wanted to harvest any for ourselves. Our children spent hours picking berries. We would have been worried about them, had it not been for the big Saint Bernard I had purchased on the way home from our wedding. This dog adored our kids and never left their side except for a brief interlude with a bunch of pigs that he had adopted as his own! (More on them elsewhere in the book). Even with the dog's infatuation with pigs, I never had the slightest doubt that this dog would have given his life to protect our children. Sometimes the kids would get annoyed with Jed because he got between them and vehicles and company that drove in. They wanted to be the ones to greet the visitors!

One time my sister, Ramona, was at home alone. She heard a scratching sound on the bedroom wall, so climbed up to look out the window. She nearly froze in fear when she saw a very large black bear down below. Her daughter, Lisa, lived about 100 yards away. She too was alone, except for her Airdale dogs. Ramona saw the bear heading in that direction, so she grabbed the phone and called to warn her. Lisa was getting ready to take a bath and wasn't the least bit concerned about a bear being outside! She "had the dogs inside with her," and was annoyed at even being warned of any danger! She calmly went ahead with her nice bubble bath. Suddenly she saw a large furry face staring at her through the window! That was the end of her perfectly calm attitude. Had the dogs been outside, the bear wouldn't have been so brave. The girls phoned a neighbor, who came over to shoot the bear. By that time, though, it had gone further on down the trail; it's mission of being a 'peeping Tom' accomplished! This particular bear had previously left his large muddy prints on the outside of Jim and Ramona's house. She had blamed the mess on Jim and just could'nt figure out why he would smear mud off his 'gloved' hands onto the wall! Jim vehemently denied doing it!

One summer, I had gotten twenty acres worked up and needed the roots picked before it was ready to seed. Because I was working other land, a half mile away, Wilma took all four kids and headed down to pick, pile and burn roots. She had such a strong feeling that she was being watched; yet she could see nothing or no one. The feeling was so strong, her nerves finally compelled her to load up the kids and head for home. She glanced back, when driving away, and a large black bear came out from the bush and on to the field. Wilma went to get my Dad. He got the gun and drove the vehicle, with the kids still in the back. As they got close, the bear started to run away. Dad punched the accelerator and took off after it; forgetting about the kids. As they bounced over ditches and clumps of sod, he was losing kids with every bump! Wilma was aggravated at him, but he did get the bear! And of course, we retrieved the kids! It was the largest bear we had ever shot out there. It had been laying down, just inside the trees, watching them the entire time they were working.

Bears are extremely powerful; especially in their arms. If one ever swats you, it's likely to be fatal. One time I was standing on the shore of the McKenzie River at Ft. Simpson when I saw one swimming across from the opposite bank. The river is over a mile wide. When he got to our side, some Indian children spotted him and began to throw rocks at him. The bear turned around and swam back to the other side. After awhile, he seemed to remember why he wanted to be on our side. He swam all the way back, landing about a mile downstream. He shook himself off like a dog and walked up the bank; disappearing into the thick brush. That bear had just just swam well over three miles and didn't seem to be the least bit fatigued.

In 1955, I worked all one winter and into the summer in the Swan Hills, north of Edmonton. That was before any oil activity had begun there. It is in this area that the largest true Grizzly bears in North America have been located. It is presumed they are remnants of the ones who used to follow the buffalo herds in the days of Lewis and Clark. The world record used to be held by an Indian woman who shot it with a '22 single shot rifle. It is said that her husband had climbed a tree to escape. Because of her arthritis she couldn't climb, so was forced to shoot. Apparently she hit the bear in the eye and the bullet penetrated its brain. The head of the bear was on display in a little town on the south shore of Lesser Slave Lake for many years. For all I know, it may still be there. The big bears used to come over to our area, but farming and oil activity drove them away. I saw one on our homestead years ago, when checking out a fire guard with my neighbor, Bill Goad. My first impression was that it was a brown colored cow, until it hit me that no one around there had cattle at the time. On closer examination, we realized it was a Grizzley, and a very big one at that! I was so stunned at the sight, that I just stood there and let him walk off. We were within fifty yards of this bear when he disappeared into the bush. It amazed me that an oldtimer, like

Billl Goad, was afraid of guns. To my knowledge, he never owned one.

Thank you for "bearing" with me. This chapter on "Bear Tails" has gotten a lot longer than a bear's tail!

THE GREAT SQUIRREL DOG

Our st Bernard was a huge mass of muscle and a wonderful pet, but just a tad bit short in the brain department. Don't get me wrong. We loved that lazy old hound. Maybe he was smarter than we thought, but it seemed he did everything backwards. For instance, if you sent him after a wandering cow, he would charge off with loads of enthusiasm until he got to the cow. Then he would stand in front of it and bark until the cow lowered her head and charged him. At this point, he would run towards us with the cow just inches from his tail. It served the purpose, but it sure looked crazy! I guess he wasn't in any danger of getting kicked in the head that way. What seemed to infuriate the cow, was that the dog ran, looking over his shoulder, with a big grin on his slobbery face. When he got close, he would make a sharp turn and then look at you as if to say, "Well, here she is! What did you want her for?"

Jed's greatest passion was squirrels though; with field mice running a close second. Her Majesty (the cat) kept him well supplied with rabbits, so he didn't have to chase them. Every morning throughout the winter she would have four or five lined up in front of our door for him to breakfast on.

I think the reason Jed hated squirrels so much stemmed back to the time I shot one out of a tree in our front yard. As it fell out of the top of the tree, Jed bounded up to grab it. He quickly discovered it wasn't quite dead! It sunk its teeth into Jed's nose and died, still hanging on like that. Jed was squealing and snapping his slobbery head around trying to dislodge it. It couldn't let go. Finally he put his big old paw on it and tore out a chunk of his own nose in the process. Ever since then he held a grudge against squirrels.

He seemed to be very put out that they could climb trees and he couldn't. Even though he did try hard, gravity always took over. That wasn't surprising, considering his great weight.

We had an old log barn a couple hundred yards from the house. A couple squirrels had taken up residence in the rafters. Jed knew about these critters, but was at a great disadvantage because they were much faster than he was. They always got up on the rafters before he could nab them.

For you to appreciate this "squirrel tale" I need to describe this barn to you. As I mentioned, it was made of log. During our first year on the homestead, we threshed wheat and blew the straw on the flat roof. This actually made a good cover and even shed rain if the kids didn't get up there and disturb it. Most of the chinking had fallen out, so on a hot summer day it was nice and cool inside.

We left the door open so the horses could go in and escape the flies and heat.

One hot day in August, my Dad and I wandered down there to get out of the heat. There were several horses inside; all in various stages of sleepiness. Dad and I stood there, talking quietly. We were almost whispering because it was so still and peaceful. We saw Jed come hurtling down the road. Evidently he thought that we had gone to the pasture without him, and was hurrying to catch up. Just as he was passing the barn door, he remembered the squirrels and took a flying leap through the door. At the same time he let go with one of his deafening barks. He was hoping to catch the squirrels sleeping.

You may have heard the expression "loud enough to wake the dead." That describes perfectly what happened. One moment it was peacefully quiet with the horses standing hipshot, and Dad and I whispering to each other, so as not to break the spell. Then ... PANDEMONIUM!" Horses and dogs and squirrels all running for their lives! We never could figure how we escaped being trampled in the rush! I looked outside and there were the horses running at a dead gallop, with Jed stretched out in the lead! He was running low to the ground, just tearing up the sod! The two squirrels were on the corral rails scolding everything in general! Inside the barn the dust was sifting down and all was quiet and peaceful once again. Dad and I were still in shock. Suddenly the realization of what had happened hit us. We began to laugh until we had to sit down on the manger to keep from falling down. Eventually Jed came wandering back, looking mighty sheepish. This time he didn't even look for the squirrels. He just flopped down in the dirt and wagged his tail.

We cut the grain with a binder and put it in "shocks" (if you are American). If you are English or Canadian you'd call them "stooks." This required grabbing a bundle under each arm and standing them up against each other. After doing this with four to six more bundles, you had a complete "stook." This procedure allowed the grain to dry until a threshing machine was brought in to harvest the grain.

Dad and I were out in the field "stooking." Jed was roaming around, hunting mice. Suddenly he spotted one and tore after it like a run away freight train. The mouse darted between Dad's legs, with Jed in hot pursuit. Because Jed weighed two hundred and five pounds, he knocked Dad spinning! Dad was just getting back to his feet when the mouse made a fast u-turn and ran under him for protection. This time Jed landed with both feet in the pit of Dad's stomach and knocked the breath out of him! Dad began to yell his favorite expression at the dog - which would have been **"You crazy knothead,"** but all that came out was a wheezy little sound. It didn't mean anything, but I knew what it was supposed to be.

Dad seemed to be a little upset with me for laughing, but I couldn't seem to stop. I did feel kind of sorry for him though. After all, he was my Father. One thing I was pretty sure of was - if the situation had been reversed, he might have had a stroke laughing at me! That would have been sad. So it was probably a good thing it happened like it did.

Jed thought he was a member of the family and expected to be treated as such. When we went down to check on the cows in winter, he would come up behind us and hold his paw up to our hand. He'd just hold it there until we "held <u>his</u> hand". He would sit like that until we were ready to go back into the house. Wilma seemed to find this comforting. Somehow, she enjoyed holding his paw! I became a little jealous, but consoled myself with the fact that he refused to come in the house, so I didn't have any competition indoors! I said Jed wouldn't come in the house - but there was one exception. That was when it thundered. Then he would knock anyone down who got between him and the door! He was terrified of thunder.

When we sold the homestead and moved to Penticton, British Columbia, we took him with us. However, he caused so many traffic jams and got into so much trouble in the city that we ended up giving him away. His new owner was a rancher who had fallen in love with him. We all grieved over our loss, but we knew Jed was better off in the country.

HORSE TAILS

It has been said that everyone has a least one weakness. I know a man whose weakness is antique two-cylinder tractors ; John Deere tractors in particular. He has, however, been known to purchase a few other models. I think, in order to keep his identity secret, we'll just call him "Art." Art has been known to travel to far and distant places just to buy a part for a tractor! Sometimes he even buys miniature model tractors to display on the mantel over his wood stove.

I am reluctant to admit to any weakness of my own. Yet there are a few things that I find intriguing to the point that I might arrive home with them when I could have easily lived
without them. When we lived on the homestead, I generally had three or four horses around, when two would have been sufficient. One thing I always had plenty of was land. In fact, we had land that we couldn't afford to clear the poplar trees from! As a consequence, it sat idle and didn't make us any profit. That was always the dilemma I was faced with. There was more going out than coming in. Wilma would lovingly suggest that I take a couple horses in to the auction. The conversation would go like this: "Steve, if you think eating is necessary for your health, then I would suggest that you sell a couple of those useless nags and put that money towards some groceries!" I felt this was totally uncalled for, as we had moose and grouse just running around begging to be shot and put on the table. We even had a grinder that ground wheat almost fine enough to make flour. Our Saint Bernard dog thrived on grain and moose scraps. Admittedly, he wasn't a fussy eater, but I didn't think we should be either!

I could be heard grumbling about modern women who were "spoiled" with luxuries like sugar, salt, spices etc. Regardless, I usually did what Wilma asked. That is: I would take one in to the sale, but often ended up buying two to bring home! I couldn't help myself. So there! That is my weakness! Wilma, the smart lady that she is, recognized this early on in our marriage, and got me to sell something else instead. Periodically, I would go to work away from the farm for awhile in order to pay for these luxuries.

I recognized from childhood that all animals had distinct personalities, but none more so than horses and dogs. For instance, we had a dog who would chase coyotes or about anything. However, when asked to go into the brush after a wounded bear, he would look at me with an expression that clearly said, "Do I look stupid or something?" No amount of threats or coaxing would change his mind. Yet, when I got fed up with arguing with him and went in and killed the bear myself, he'd rush up and bite it and then look at me as if to say, "Boy! Was I brave! I sure took care of that one!"

My Dad owned a Terrier (of some undetermined breed) that our big dog chewed on and pestered unmercifully. It always looked so sad, like it was a real martyr. Once in awhile our neighbor's big dog would come visiting and always ended up in a ferocious fight with ours. This was just the opportunity Dad's Terrier was waiting for. It would dance around the edge of the fight and snap at the other two whenever the opportunity presented itself. The expression of 'sheer satisfaction' on that dog was comical to see. It really exacted its revenge when the other two were too busy to retaliate!

My old horse, Trixy, had all sorts of expressions one could read. When over-worked, she looked at me and her expression said, "Why me? Why is it always me?" Or if I had missed a throw when roping a cow, Trixy would turn her head and say, "Do I have to do everything for you?"

One of the most exasperating animals is a cow! A cow will find a hole in the fence and stand out in the alfalfa with the most innocent and dumb expression on her face. It was like they didn't know they had done anything wrong. I believe most cows have built-in attitudes that make them rebels. By this, I mean that they will decide what you want of them and do the exact opposite! I don't even want to start on a pig's idea of how to make a human go insane!

As you can probably see, animals are a lot like humans. Some are good workers with positive attitudes, while others will try your patience to the extreme. Since being away from the farm for a long time, I am of the opinion that as ornery as some animals are, they are still easier to understand than humans.

Don't get me wrong. I love almost everyone, but with animals I know pretty well what to expect.

TRIXY

I believe I entitled this chapter "Horse Tails," so maybe I should talk more about horses. I'll start with "Trixy."

Trixy was captured as a two-year old from a band of wild horses that used to run in the Chinchaga range, which is about 150 miles northwest of Peace River, Alberta. It's a very wild area composed of swamps and meadows and the dreaded muskeg. Trixy was a bg bald-faced mare with a long homely face. I guess because of her origin, she had a talent that very few horses had. She could traverse very boggy muskeg with ease. Most horses, when in soft or boggy ground, will panic. They begin to plunge and jump — only to mire themselves deeper. Trixy would stretch her front foot way out ahead and pull herself forward. We called it "cat footing." Most of her habits were good. What really endeared her to us was her way with chiildren. Our kids could do anything with her. The first evidence of this was when Sandra was about six months old. Wilma was helping me build a corral. We had spread some clean straw around for Sandra to sit in. We looked around and saw Trixy's head right down sniffing at Sandra. Sandra reached up and grabbed her ears and pulled herself upright. To our surprise, the horse seemed to be enjoying it. Later when there were four children, all of them could climb on her out in the pasture. They rode her around with nothing more than a piece of binder twine. When we had company, we piled as many as six on her. If one slid off, Trixy stopped and stood absolutely still while they climbed on again.

One of her varied talents was that she seemed to sense when a hard job was coming up. This was when she was hard to catch! I tried to tempt her with a pail of oats, but she just ignored me. Finally, I'd go inside and send Sandra or Stephen out. They could walk right up to her with a piece of twine and she would lower her head for them to slip it on.

Trixy had one trait that was both amusing or annoying, according to the circumstance. She had to be the boss of a herd, and with no exceptions. She could put the fear of God into any horse that even presumed to take her position. This way, she always got the best feed and the choicest patch of grass to be found. I liked to feed all the horses some oats occasionally, so they would be easier to catch when I needed them. If I had four horses, I had to spread four feed boxes around the corral, so Trixy wouldn't get it all.

In the town of Valleyview, all the horse lovers in the community came together on Saturday and had gymkhana events. It was family oriented and lots of fun. One event I expecially liked was stock horse racing. Trixy was competitive to the extreme and generally got off to a fast start. When another horse began to pull up alongside her, she would give it the evil eye. If that didn't work, she'd bare her teeth at the competitor and it would fall back in its 'proper' place. One big thoroughbred gelding actually skidded to a halt, nearly causing a pile up. This didn't endear me too much with the other participants -- bunch a cry babies they were! Because of things like this, I had to quit racing her.

One day Wilma and I were out riding just for the pleasure of it. We came out of the woods to the edge of a freshly plowed field. It was a half mile to the other end. At the far end, I had cleared 60 acres of poplar. The fallen trees were lying criss-crossed all over like jackstraws. I was riding a nice Morgan named Flicka, who was unbelievably fast. Not only that, but she could go from a standing start so fast she almost left you sitting in mid-air. I suggested a race, and Wilma quickly agreed. She was sure Trixy would use her 'evil eye' to intimidate my horse, but I had a trick up my sleeve. Flicka could jump out in the lead and her fear of that evil demon behind her would keep her in front. (The evil demon being Trixy - not Wilma!) It worked perfectly. I got a good lead and all Flicka needed was to hear the monster behind her. That inspired her to run like the devil was on her heels! I saw the piled trees and tried to pull up, or at least turn, but Flicka would

106

have none of it. She feared Trixy far more than the tangled mess in front of her so she plunged staight in. Of course she tripped and we flew end over end through the air, with both of us landing flat on our backs. I don't know about Flicka, but even though it was mid-day, I could see stars circling around in the sky overhead! About that time, Trixy flashed past with her teeth bared and giving that look of hers! I believe she was saying, "Serves you right, you smart alec!"

We decided to ride the horses home from Valleyview one day, which was a distance of 28 miles. Wilma was on Trixy and I rode Comet, a big gelding. As usual, Trixy had to be a half-length ahead, and this was annoying me to no end. I eased my foot out of the stirrup and gave her a kick in the tail section. Big mistake!! She leapt ahead sideways so fast it nearly unseated Wilma. She aimed a kick at Comet, just missing my leg. Now I not only had to ride in the rear, I also had Wilma upset with me! Wilma looked at me with that hurt look in her eyes that always made me feel guilty - even when I wasn't. Trixy just gave me the evil eye that made me keep plenty of space between myself and her.

Another time, Wilma and my Dad went out looking for some stray cattle. For some reason they switched horses, so Dad was riding Trixy. Wilma didn't like riding in the rear anymore than I did. There is something uninspiring when the only view is that of a horse's rear end! Wilma tried to pull alongside Dad and Trixy turned and bit her on the leg. When she screamed, Comet spun around and kicked Dad on his leg. Of course the horses were trying to punish each other, but managed to target the rider instead. Dad and Wilma both came limping home that night.

Trixy would do almost any task she was put to. She could be worked in harness, packed; and I've even skidded moose out of the woods with the saddle horn. Carl and Glen Hatch (from Stayton, Oregon) were up one fall hunting moose. Each had managed to bag one northeast of my homestead. However, as is so often the case, they were in a swampy area where you couldn't get a vehicle in anywhere close. I took Trixy over and tied a rope from the saddle horn to the moose and started leading her. I was up to my knees in the water when we came to a beaver run that was about four feet deep. I paused to plan a way around, but Trixy bumped into me, knocking me down. She skidded that moose right over me! By the time I pulled myself out, she had gotten to dry ground without me. She looked as me as if to say, "What were you doing? Taking a nap?"

One thing I want to make clear is that I never was a great cowboy, although Wilma thought I was. I did what I could, and learned a little here and there. None of our horses were great cutting horses either. They all had traits that made them good for specific jobs. Flicka was so quick that she should have made a good cutting horse, but everything was like a race to her. You'd go after a cow that had broken away from the herd and she'd catch up with it in a flash; but fly right on by. Each time we'd swing around, she would do the same thing again. She had a gait that was as smooth as silk and it was a pleasure to use for trail riding. However, she never learned to handle cattle. I eventually sold her to a man who was a great horseman, and she went on to win money in barrel racing.

Our main pasture consisted of about 500 acres of meadows with thick clumps of willows scattered here and there. All together, the willows took up about 5 acres of space. Willow clumps were a nice place for the cows to get away from pesky flies, or just to give some shade on a hot day. They were a real pain though when we were trying to bring a cow back to the corral. The cows would make a dash for the willows, and it was near torture to run through them. Trixy was the only horse that could do it well, but she had no regard for the man on her back! She would figure out which cow we were after - bare her teeth - and the cow would run for dear life - Trixy right on her tail. Usually the cow would think she could excape by running into the willows, but that didn't deter Trixy one iota! She just lowered her head and charged in after it. All the rider could do was lift his feet out of the stirrups and (with eyes closed) lay out flat on her back, with a tight grip on the saddle horn! Sometimes it worked - sometimes it didn't! When the cow came out on the other side, Trixy was right on her tail. Likely as not, she'd bite the cow on the rump, just to remind her who was in charge. Those bites were painful and would take a four-inch patch of hair right off the fleeing cow. It usually only took one time, and the cow was educated! Of course, like people, a few needed to further their education! I lost a lot of hats in those willow clumps.

I picked a Bay gelding up from the French settlement of Falher. It was during the time Pierre Trudeau was Prime Minister, so we named him Pierre. The horse was a perfect gentleman as soon as one got a rope on him, but he was a crafty thing. He was almost impossible to catch out in the open. When I had plans to use him, I either had to keep him penned up or on a picket. He was smooth to ride and quite good with cattle, but I had to keep a

108

good grip on the reins. If I got off to open a gate and was even the slightest bit careless, it would take two or three hours to catch him again. When I put oats in the corral for the horses, Pierre would stand outside and watch the others eat until he saw I was a fair distance away. That way he took a chance of not being caught. When I was through with him for awhile, I'd lead him to the gate and very carefully begin to remove the halter. When Pierre thought it was loose, he'd nearly tear my arm off getting away! He would have been a perfect stock horse if it weren't for his fear of the handler.

Sandra and Stephen grew to be a lot of help with the cattle and they loved to help, especially if the task involved riding a horse. I always had them ride Trixy because she was so trustworthy. Sandra didn't mind falling and getting skinned up, but Stephen feared humiliation. I guess it was because the Lusch family has always been bad for teasing, and of course he didn't like being laughed at. One day he was galloping Trixy around and around our house; all the time swinging a lariat. He was trying to rope a chair that was sitting in the yard. He had the lariat tied to the saddle horn and when he came around again, he made a perfect throw and connected. When he galloped on past, the chair flew up and smacked Trixy hard in the rump, then it bounced along behind. Trixy evidently thought a demon was out to get her, because she really stretched out and headed for pasture! When she came to the gate, she jumped right over it, bouncing Stephen off against the gatepost in the process! The rest of us were laughing and yelling at him for letting go and falling off. Stephen, in return, made no response. He was lying very still on the ground as Trixy made a big circle around the field with the chair still bouncing on behind. Wilma was on the run to where her son lay. She said some very uncomplimentary things about me and the kids laughing, and not realizing that Stephen was hurt. The word "Stupid" seems to stand out in my mind. (By the way, Wilma, you never have apologized for those things you called me.) Stephen was unconscious and scratched up some, but he soon came around and seemed more concerned about falling off than he was about being hurt. Later on, when I wanted to get his dander up, I would tell someone (in his presence) that Stephen had 'accidently' roped the chair. He would get very upset with me. He was about ten years old at the time.

I had a tall, part thoroughbred gelding when Sandra was three. It had not been broke to ride, but was tame as a kitten. We used to put Sandra on him and he would walk alongside us when

109

we went riding; Sandra would have a tight grip on his mane. One evening, we all rode down to my parent's house, which was 3/4 of a mile away from our place. The young gelding trotted ahead as we came into Mom and Dad's yard. Sandra was laughing and having a great time. Mom happened to glance out the window and see her. Thinking Sandra was alone, she ran outside. When the screen door slammed behind her, the horse spooked and jumped right out from under Sandra. She was sitting on the ground screaming at the top of her lungs, and we were sure she was hurt. When we got to her, she just screamed, "I want back on! I want back on!" She was furious because she had fallen off. Of course I got a lecture from my Mother, about allowing a little child to ride an unbroken horse. No matter how badly Sandra got skinned up, she was always game to try again. She had no fear, and 'humiliation' was not in her vocabulary!

One day I came home with a Shetland pony, thinking the kids would have a lot of fun with it. The auctioneer read the manifest to the crowd, which said: "Any child can ride this pony! It is well broke and gentle." I was anxious for our kids to try it out, and Brenda was the first to have the honor. I rigged it up, sat her on it and let go. The horse went running and bucking out across the field, with Brenda hanging on for dear life. Fortunately, there was about 18 inches of snow on the ground, so when she fell, she would have somewhat of a cushion to land on. I happened to have the tractor running at the time, so I jumped on it and soon caught up to the runaway horse, which was now nearly a mile away and with rider still intact! By this time, she was hanging off-side and about ready to ditch it. I got them both home and then got on the pony myself. I intended to give it some education, but the ignorant thing wouldn't stop bucking, even though my feet could touch the ground at every jump. I was furious as I stepped off. I am ashamed to admit this, but I swung my fist at its head. Just at that moment, the pony threw his head up, and I broke a bone in my hand. This was Saturday.

The next day, Sunday, we went to church as always. Wouldn't you know, the lesson was on "Forgiveness and turning the other cheek." That subject made it a little awkward to explain how I broke my hand. It seemed everybody in the church tried to shake my hand that particular morning! It had swollen to about the size of a small cantalope. If I had known what the lesson was, I might have stayed home!

This time, I listened to my wife and a month later I sold that little outlaw. And..I didn't bring any more horses home! I didn't even stay for the auction. Just in case you are wondering, "No." I did not put anything on the manifest about how 'well broke' he was! However, this was not the last I saw of that pony. An old cowboy from Texas was at the sale and he bought it to give to my friend, Arne Johnson for his kids! This old-timer was named Milsap. (I wish someone would write a book about him!) All he would say about his past was that he could not return to Texas! He lived back in the bush in a little cabin and did just enough trapping and horse trading to keep beans on the table. He was a frequent visitor at Arne's home. Arne was a much better cowboy than I was, but he didn't have any better luck with that little knothead of a pony than I had. Eventually it ended up back at the auction and hopefully in someone's canned dog food!

In the 1990's, Sandra and I had 80 acres along the highway north of Valleyview. You guessed it! We had a half dozen horses! One of them was a buckskin mare we called Lady. Her registered name was "Old Miss Horton." From the registration papers, she was just two generations away from the most famous Quarter horse of all time, "Three Bars." She was old for a working horse when I got her, but she was beautiful and lively. She also seemed to know what a cow was going to do before the cow had even decided. I got two colts from her before we moved back to Oregon, and had to sell her. As far as I know, both colts turned out to be great cow ponies. The first one won $50,000. in barrel racing, as a three-year old.

One day I returned home to find Lady bleeding profusely; her leg over a barbwire fence just below her pastern. When I got her foot off the wire, it was cut through the main artery and blood was spurting out about a distance of ten feet. I didn't know what to do except to clean it and pack it with salve. Then I wrapped it tightly to stop the bleeding. Lady stood there and held her foot up for me to work on. She seemed to understand that I was trying to help her. I was over fifty years old, but I could hardly keep from crying. It was a weekend and the only veterinarian in the area was ninty miles away, in Peace River. They were closed for the day! The Vet said he would see her on Sunday morning. We were waiting when he arrived at the clinic. He sedated her; took off the bandages; cleaned the wounds and stitched them up. He told me that·I had done the best thing possible for her. She recovered fairly quickly, but the tendon had been damaged, leaving her with a limp. She couldn't be used for work, but the kids rode her around the acreage. She was later sold to a man for his children to ride; and to raise another colt.

There was a beautiful buckskin in a pasture on the way to Grande Prairie. I admired that horse everytime I drove by it, but had no idea who owned her. One day I was at the Lumber yard and got talking to the owner about horses. It turned out to be his horse. Eventually I bought her from him. I hadn't even ridden her, so I left her in the corral while I went back to town. I warned Sandra's kids to stay out of the corral, because a new horse was not to be trusted until one got to know it. They didn't obey me any more than their mother did! As I returned home that afternoon, I saw someone riding in the hay yard. When I got out of the pickup and walked out there, who should it be but Tricia riding bare back with just a twine on the horse's nose. She was backing her around hay bales. I didn't know whether to be mad or proud! Tricia would have been about ten years old then.

Sandra had a beautiful Palomino mare that was a bit nervous and head shy. But, for all that, she was a nice, smooth riding horse. We hoped to get a colt from her, even though she was about 18 years old. However, I talked to her former owner and learned that they had tried for years to have her bred, but with no success. I had been boarding a nice Stallion, so I went ahead and let nature take its course. The next Spring, she showed no sign of being pregnant, so we removed her to a rented pasture 30 miles away. Four days later, I came by to check on her. Following her around was the scrawniest little colt I'd ever seen! She never had much milk so the colt didn't grow very fast. This was probably due to her age and never having had a colt before.

This chapter has gotten twice as long as I'd planned. Let it suffice to say, we had some very interesting experiences with horses! May all but the Shetland find good pasture in the great horse pasture in the sky! (Well, maybe him too -- if he repented!)

112

THE COW TAIL

Raising cattle is one of the most pleasurable ways I know to lose money. I had just spent a couple very profitable winters working in the Northwest Territories (in northern Canada) and had come home to join my sweet wife and four children on our homestead in Fish Creek, Alberta. My dream had been to be a cattle rancher, and now I had the opportunity to achieve it.

A cattle rancher near Westlock had 45 cows with calves at foot for sale. I quickly phoned him to see if we could make a deal. I had acquired a tandem grain truck and my plan was to trade it as partial payment on the cattle. He was agreeable and even wanted a load of feed oats if I had any; which I did. The year before, I had planted fifteen acres of newly cleared land, which had produced one of the heaviest crops I'd ever seen. I had lots of oats but the grain dealers weren't buying just then. I loaded 600 bushels on the truck and hit the road before daylight, arriving in Westlock about ten a.m. The man loved the truck. He climbed up to look at the oats and came down shaking his head. He said, "Son, those are the finest and cleanest oats I have ever seen. It would be a crime to use them for feed." I explained that they were the only kind I had, and that I had lots more at home. I encouraged him to take them, as per our agreement. He thought about it for a minute and agreed to do it; but he insisted on throwing in two skinny cows. They appeared to be barren. He thought maybe I could fatten them up for butchering later in the year. He was an honest man, and didn't want to cheat me. Also he offered to brand them for me right then and there, if I had a brand. He promised to deliver them to me right away. I was delighted, because I hadn't thought of branding them, and didn't have the facilities anyway. With his large crew, we had the job done before lunch and I was ready to go home. We separated the cows from the calves and loaded them into two trucks. I climbed in with one trucker, and we were off.

We arrived home at about six p.m. and unloaded in the home pasture. First we unloaded the calves, and then the cows to mother-up with their babies. This pasture was only about ten acres; just right for this process. I had been in such a hurry to get the cattle, I hadn't fenced more than the 10 acres. Wilma, my Dad and I got busy the following morning, driving fence posts and stringing wire.

We had about 300 acres of wild pasture to fence, so were extremely busy for about a week. During that time I lost two calves to "shipping fever," because I wasn't able to check them soon enough. This pasture was low land that was under water early in the spring - thanks to a family of busy beavers, who kept damming up the creek. It was green before anything else had gotten a start. Several clumps of willows clustered around it, making it excellent pastureland. In fact, a few years later a neighbor had run low on grass, so I let him turn in about 60 head with mine. We pastured 140 cows with calves for a full summer, and the pasture could have taken another fifty.

Wilma and I eventually drove in the last staple, and just in time too. The home pasture was eaten down pretty close to the dirt. The cows were getting that look in their eyes that said something about "the grass being greener on the other side." We learned quickly that a cow doesn't really need a reason to go through a fence. They do it just to aggravate you! Then they stare at you with that innocent look, like they had no idea they weren't supposed to be on the opposite side of the fence! Although I sincerely love cattle, they are without question, the most contrary creatures on the face of the earth!

We found a cow in the herd that we thought might make a good milk cow. I got a rope and skidded her home behind my old horse, Trixy. The reason I say "skidded", is because she immediately began to show her true nature, and planted her feet in the dirt. She refused to move in any direction except the opposite way I wanted to take her. I had already put a heavy halter on her, so I let Trixy stretch the cow's neck about as far as it could possibly go. Even then, she slid along behind, fighting every foot of the way! I tied her to a tree in our yard and went looking for a milk pail. She seemed highly insulted with all this indignity, and had apparently decided it **wasn't** gonna happen! Now I am definitely not a stubborn person. (You can ask anyone.) I knew, however, that it **was** 'gonna happen' and proceeded to educate this cow! First she needed a name, so I could yell her name, and not just call her "stupid cow!" The kids agreed unanimously that her name would be "Bossy." That was one hurdle surmounted. The rest proved to be a little more difficult. I did have enough experience with cows to tie her back legs up. I had been slapped in the face with a soggy tail enough times to secure that too! I then proceeded to position the bucket under her where it would do the most good. My next step was reaching in and gripping her by the milk spouts. Then I began the normal pulling.

First she let out a sorrowful kind of moan - then a beller - then she tried to kick. When all of that failed, she just laid over on her side, pinning me underneath! Talk about indignity. Worst of all was the sound of Wilma and the kids giggling. I didn't think holding a thousand pound cow on my lap was the least bit funny, but they seemed to. When my sweet family had recovered from their amusement, I got them to untie her legs and get me out from underneath her. I then spoke very kindly to Bossy and said, **"The Good Book states that I shouldn't smite thee, and it also says I shouldn't kick thee, but it doesn't say I cannot twist thy tail!"** I proceeded right then to do just that. It didn't improve her attitude one bit!

I started the process all over again, and eventually got about a half gallon of milk from her. If you counted my time at five dollars an hour, that first milk cost me about five dollars a quart. She was one of the cows whose calf had died, so at least I didn't have to share the milk with a calf.

Let me give you another example of Bossy's plan to ruin my life. Eventually we had a small barn to milk her in. This made the chore a little simpler. At least I could tie her tail to a rafter so she couldn't lie down on me again, without pulling it off. The best grass was a couple hundred yards from the barn, so that was where we picketed her. To get her to the barn, there was a gate to open and close. There were usually two or three horses inside the fence, just waiting for the opportunity to escape. I would start by putting the rope over my shoulder and straining with all my strength to reach to gate. Bossy would do her part by pulling back, trying to make it impossible for me to do so. I would reach

115

up to unlatch the gate and crack it open just enough to get her through. She would suddenly change her strategy and charge through, trying to knock me off my feet before I could close it. I am absolutely certain she knew exactly what she was doing, and spent her idle time chewing her cud and planning new ways to torment me. She also stored up all the green grass from the whole day and didn't release it until she was in the stall. Even then, she held it until I sat down and started milking her. I would step back and wait until she was through. Just when I sat down again, she had another bodily function that she used. We milked her until just before her next calf was born. I then let the calf have her. Good riddance!

Later I picked up a Holstein heifer at the auction. The kids named her Bossy too. (Bossy the 2nd). Although she was a little better, she was far from perfect. My Dad said I was lucky because trouble was a great character builder and we needed that!

I eventually bought a little jersey cow. You could walk out in the pasture and milk her without even tying her up. She was so sweet and gentle, it was almost boring. Her name? You ask. Bossy, of course!

In June of that year I introduced a big handsome bull to the cows and romance was in the air. He was kept extremely busy and I knew it was expecting a lot, but the next spring he was daddy to 47 calves! Part of the credit for that number went to those two "barren" cows. During the first part of July, those cows both had healthy calves. I didn't need to butcher them after all.

The cattle kept our entire family involved and the kids were a big help. That winter I had to go out working again and the feeding was pretty much left up to Wilma and Stephen. I had stacked the bales of hay next to the feeders and they did the feeding and watering by themselves. Stephen was pretty small then; about nine years old. He was a big help and very dependable.

The days are short in the Peace River country in the winter. It was dark when the kids got on the school bus, and dark when they got home. They traveled a distance of 28 miles each way. Sometimes the twins, who were seven, would fall asleep on the way home. We were blessed with a good and dependable bus driver, Henry Bradley, and had no cause for worry. He put his own two-way radio in his bus years before the school district installed them in the busses. Our oldest daughter, Sandra, seldom fell asleep on the bus. She was too full of mischief. (She inherited this trait from her mother.) Sandra was a big help both in the

116

house and outdoors. Her only problem was that she was not afraid of anything.

One night our good friends and neighbors, the Hardmans, were visiting us. Sandra heard Bud remark that if a mad cow were to charge you, the best thing to do was to stand your ground and stare her down. There is some truth to this, but Bud was teasing Wilma because a cow (with a newborn calf) had run her out of the corral that day. About a week later, Sandra spotted a calf laying up by the hay while it's mom was down at the watering trough. She wandered up there and was petting the calf, when we heard the cow let out a snort. We saw it tearing up there like a runaway freight train! All of us were yelling for Sandra to run for the fence, but she just planted her little fists on her hips and glared at it. The cow skidded to a halt with its nose just inches from Sandra's face, blowing slobber all over her. We rescued her from the danger and asked her why she didn't run? She replied, **"Because Bud said to just stare them down."**

About the same time, I found where our tamest cow had dropped a calf right into a snow drift. Not expecting any problems with her, I picked the calf up, turned around and started for the barn, where I could lay it in a drier spot. The next thing I knew, I was flying through the air and landed about 20 feet away. I learned that you should always keep the calf between yourself and the cow. Motherhood will turn a quiet, placid cow into a raging maniac.

That winter, I was away for about 3 months without getting home. When I did, I drove the Oil Company's truck, which I was supposed to deliver in town for another man to pick up. That first night the kids just hung on me. The next morning when I headed out to the truck, Sandra and Stephen stood back with eyes all teary. Rebecca and Brenda wrapped their arms around my legs and started bawling. That's when I decided I wouldn't spend any more winters away from home. They thought I was leaving again. It made me a little damp around the eyes too.

In the Spring we needed to treat the cattle for Warbles. Alberta is basically warble free, and they wanted to keep it that way. I rounded up the whole family, including Mom and Dad, to help me get the cattle into the corral. I hadn't built any wings on the corral, so this was a difficult job. We got the bunch started into the corral when the leaders balked. That began a rebellious reaction with the ones in the back. They showed strong indication that they wanted to bolt back out to the pasture. All eight of us were yelling and waving ropes and sticks to persuade them to move forward before we lost the whole herd. Becky, who was seven then, ran up behind a cow with a short stick. She whacked it on the rump with all her strength. The cow simply raised her tail and let fly with a stream of fresh green manure! Its' aim was perfect (depending on one's point of view) and it hit Becky square in the face, completely covering her face; then running down the front of her shirt. Becky dropped her stick, and squalling at the top of her lungs, began clawing the stuff out of her eyes. **"Why me! Why me!"** None of us dared go to her aid, lest the cows make a break for it. So we just told her to go down to the pond and try to clean herself up as best she could. Becky took a lot of teasing after that; about why she had such a good complexion, etc. It seemed that she did have a better complexion that the rest of us!

I wanted to patent this process for the rest of the world's women who want to remove zits and other blemishes. My mother, though, advised me against it! Even Becky said she wouldn't endorse it. Another chance at riches shot down!

WITTY INVENTIONS
(Not yet proven)

Here is another little hint for the suffering public. If you have a problem with baldness, try rubbing fresh chicken manure on your head. Leave it there for a week, before removing it. You will find that you have a full head of hair. This has never been tested under laboratory conditions, but so far as I know, it has never been disproven either! If you have a cold sore, try rubbing a small amount of the same substance on the sore. It may not cure it, but it is guaranteed to stop you from licking your lips! I have never been able to get anyone to volunteer as a test subject, so I guess these cures will be forever lost to science

A CURE FOR FAILING EYE SIGHT

I have debated with myself about imparting another little gem of knowledge about a cure for failing eyesight. This has been tested on livestock. My hesitation is because of an organization called "The Animal Rights." They frown on this sort of thing. However, I'm working on another group that we'll call "The Cattleman's Rights"; or perhaps we should entitle it "How to keep from going insane while raising cattle." Let me explain it to you.

One summer day, a troublemaking cow had found a hole in the fence and was out in the wheat field. She had that idiotic, innocent look on her face that used to infuriate me. I spent a good half hour chasing her past the hole in the fence, trying to get her back through it. She couldn't seem to see it, even though she had just crawled out in the opposite direction. My vast store of patience was about depleted when my dad drove in the yard. He claimed to have a secret weapon that was guaranteed to improve a cow's eyesight. It involved some 'twelve gauge' shotgun shells loaded with rock salt. Even though I didn't approve of the sound of this plan, I was completely out of breath from chasing that cow. I gave in and gave him the green light to give it a try. The results were astounding. Without the slightest hesitation, and with a great deal of speed, she saw the hole in the fence and was through it in a flash! She was making tracks for the middle of the pasture.

Science probably has a technical solution for this riddle. However I came to the conclusion that the salt, applied just under the skin, caused certain enzymes to rush to the cow's head, thus clearing up her eyesight. Previously, she had been unable to see the hole. Immediately after the rock salt treatment, she could see it clearly! Amazing!! Just one more bit of advise for you young people: If you do try this, don't let the Animal Rights Activists hear of it.

We had a lot more adventures with our cattle, but I knew in time I would have to make a profit. The sad reality is that no matter how much you enjoy any occupation, it must create some revenue or you have to take on another job to support the first! This is the situation I eventually found myself in. Cattle that I had paid four hundred dollars a pair for, were now bringing only two hundred. I tried to weather the storm for about three years, but eventually had to face reality and dispose of them before they disposed of me!

Ironically, the year after I sold out, prices started climbing and went way up to as much as a thousand dollars a pair. Hindsight is always better than foresight. Eventually we sold the homestead too, and moved to British Columbia to pastor a church.

Even though this venture had not panned out, I still look back on it as one of the happiest times of my life. We were young and optimistic. Our children were healthy, and we did so many things together as a family. Money was always scarce, but our garden grew an abundant crop every year and moose walked right by our front door begging to be shot and put in the deep freeze. Sometimes I would oblige them, but other times I had to disappoint them because the deep freeze was full - or it was out of season. Some people actually shot them out of season! Yes, I was appalled at this violation of ethics too.

This article has gotten rather lengthy, so I think I'll cut this cow tail off right here. (A little cowboy humor there).

THIS IS THE END OF THE COW'S TAIL!

CURIOSITY ALMOST KILLED THE CAT

Wilma said the cat must be dead. She had been gone for two days. We had called "Here Kitty, here Kitty" until our throats were hoarse, and still no Kitty. The kids said the 'explosion' had killed her. Then suddenly, she appeared on the front porch; seemingly unharmed. That is, if you didn't count her deafness. It seemed the explosion had affected her hearing. That, of course, was why she hadn't heard us calling. Like all cats, she only came when it suited her; at her convenience and certainly not ours! I called her "Your Highness" because she thought she owned the place and considered us to be her "loyal subjects." In her way of thinking, we were only there to serve her. When she didn't need us, we could do whatever we desired with our time.

We wanted an original name for this cat, so we named her "Kitty!" Because of the many coyotes and owls around, we had a difficult time keeping cats for long. So, when this big Calico showed up one day, the kids began to pamper her until she thought it was her due. She was a great hunter and really earned her keep. Better yet, she gave birth to a litter of kittens every few months. After I watched her put the run on the neighbor's German Shepherd, I realized why the coyotes didn't bother her.

I was on the combine's platform, working on the ignition switch, when the neighbor's dog wandered in and saw me there. He meandered over, after leaving his calling card on several trees around the yard. Standing up, with paws on the platform, he examined the work I was doing. I halfway expected him to offer some advise on the job, but he just stood there with his tongue hanging out. Ignitions must not have been his area of expertise; or he was tired from visiting his girl friend over at Hardman's ranch. He would have been living on borrowed time if our St Bernard had been home, but that dumb dog had taken it upon himself to look after the pigs. No doubt he (Jed) was leading them somewhere, as seemed to be his pattern.

Now Jed was very particular about who watered the trees around our yard, and wouldn't put up with another mutt moving in on his territory. About this time, I noticed the cat going into her stalking mode. I just sat back to see what she was up to. She sneaked quietly around the back of the combine and I knew immediately there would be some real live drama forthcoming! Suddenly the dog's eyeballs rolled back in his head. He stood straight up on his hind legs and let out a mournful howl before toppling over backwards. Kitty had dug her front claws into his exposed stomach, and was raking that tender area with her hind claws. By the time the poor dog had gathered his wits, considerable damage had already been done. There were streaks of blood where Kitty had done her handiwork. From what I had witnessed, there was some question in my mind if that German Shepherd would be dropping in on our neighborhood in the future? He was just a brown streak as he left our yard! It appeared he had urgent business elsewhere.

Just then Jed came up the driveway with his charges - the pigs! Jed glanced around at the retreating German Shepherd, who was burning up the underbrush on his way home. Then he took in the cat - her hair standing on end. She looked twice her size and her tail stood straight up! Jed winked at her as if to say, "Way to go, Kitty! I'll do the tree watering around this yard!" I actually pitied the coyote that would be foolish enough to tackle that vicious cat.

One thing Kitty didn't understand though, was dynamite. I worked for an explosive company during the winters, supplying dynamite and other products for seismograph companies. I was Branch Manager in Fort Simpson, which is way up on the McKenzie River in the Northwest Territories. When Spring rolled around and the frost went out of the ground, these seismic crews pulled out and headed south. Any dynamite left over was returned to us and placed in our company's powder magazine. They received credit for full cases only. Any partial sticks or cases, were above inventory. I was allowed to take them home, to the farm in Fishcreek, for use in blowing stumps or anything else that needed quick removal. This is how I ended up with an explosive called Primacord. It resembled a quarter-inch rope, but blew just like dynamite. My Dad and I decided it was time to dispose of it.

A big old cottonwood tree, rotted most of the way through the base, stood about one hundred feet in front of the house. We figured this would be a perfect candidate for our experiment. I had been told that a few wraps around the tree would cut it off. But, because the tree was so large, and of no use, lots of the Primacord would be better. I wrapped about a hundred yards of cord around the trunk, attaching it to a blasting cap and fuse. Dad and I stepped back to admire our handiwork. Everything appeared to be in order, so we put a match to it and ran up near the house, taking shelter behind another tree. Just then "Her Highness" the cat, came prowling out of the brush. She saw the smoke from the fuse and went over to investigate.

We were calling "Here Kitty, here Kitty," but she chose to ignore us. Instead she paused by the tree, cocking her head like she was thinking it all over and trying to decide what to do about it. At that moment, a big ball of fire and smoke erruped from the base of the tree. Even from our distant position, the explosion was deafening. Leaves and bark were flying by our hiding place; Her Highness right in the middle of it. Her head and forelegs were stretched out in front, with the hind legs flaying in the air! She appeared to be running but her feet never touched the ground! Then she disappeared.

I recruited all four kids to search the surrounding woods for her, but she was nowhere to be found. I suggested to Wilma that "We have more kids, so our chances of finding her would be better." She gave me a look of utter disdain. She didn't seem to have any sense of shame; nor did she apologize for her attitude. As I recall, she said something like **"No cat was worth that much!"** One thing I have learned is that women and cats will do as they please. Men and dogs should just relax and get used to it. In order to keep a true perspective of ones importance, every man should have a dog who adores him and a cat that ignores him!

Two days later, who should show up but a 'stone deaf' Kitty! It was just as well she was deaf, because she never came when called anyway. Her hearing slowly returned, and a month later she was good as new.

By this time winter was closing in on us, and mornings were really frosty. Dad and I were going into town one cold morning and heard a strange "thunk" when we started the pick up. We shut the motor off and raised the hood. There was her majesty on the ground, beneath the truck. She had crawled under the hood to get warm. When the motor started, she had jumped into the fan. We pulled her lifeless body out and laid her by a tree, with intentions of burying her upon our return from town. She didn't look much like royalty with one of her eye balls hanging out. The rest of her didn't look very good either!

When we returned home that day, I got the shovel and went to dig a small grave. But the 'body' had disappeared! We just assumed that Wilma had buried her,but she assured me she hadn't. The mystery remained unsolved until a few days later. Showing up on the doorstep, was none other than Miss Royalty herself! Her eye was back in place and her wounds were healing up well. I think she stayed away until she looked presentable. After all, royalty is supposed to look proper. She didn't want us to see her as any less than 'purr-fect!'

Kitty walked up and rubbed against my legs as if nothing had ever happened. Then she sauntered over to Wilma's flower

123

bed and rolled around awhile. I guess she wanted to smell good as well as look good! If I believed in reincarnation, I think I might want to come back as a cat!

 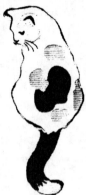

THE BIRD DOG

"If that crazy pooch points at one more bird, I swear I'm gonna scream!" I was frustrated and possibly talking louder than normal. At any rate, my good wife began backing towards the door, just in case she had to run for it! Our homestead abounded with ruffed grouse. You could see their pointed little heads poking out of the grass just about anywhere.

The aforementioned 'pooch' was a shorthaired, German Pointer, which we had inherited through no fault of our own. He was driving us insane. At the moment, he was standing in our driveway, pointing at a pair of grouse roosting in a tree. It was ten o'clock at night. He had been out there since five in the afternoon; nose aimed at the birds, tail straight back and one front leg bent at the knee. With the full moon shining down, he looked a lot like a lawn statue. I had uttered the words about the "crazy pooch" because I was sick of shooting those birds. This was the most persistent dog I'd ever seen. He would stand and point at the grouse until I took pity on him and shot the bird. Then he would look at me with adoration in his brown eyes, before trotting over and to retrieve the prize. He then laid it, as an offering, at my feet.

Normally I am an easy going guy and wouldn't get too excited about this. However, our freezer was full of birds. My sweet woman was complaining about cleaning them. She claimed this additional chore was too time consuming to add to her regular ones of splitting wood, cleaning the barn, keeping house, washing diapers and wiping the kid's snotty noses! I was getting a headache from all the complaining.

The dog had wandered into a friend's yard one day and just hung around. He had that 'lost look' about him. Beings this neighbor already had a dog, he brought this one to us. He never said anything at the time, but later divulged that the dog had about driven him crazy too. This dog was constantly one the move; trotting from our place to my parent's and back again. He had a nervous energy that made you want to kick him in the derriere. For all of you less sophisticated folk, that is a nice way to say "rear end." If you walked outside with a gun in hand, he would go berserk and charge around looking for something to point at. Our poor St. Bernard had gotten a haggard look, just trying to keep up with him.

One day I set off a charge of dynamite, trying to enlarge a water hole. Pieces of dirt and debris were landing all around. That Pointer went totally bananas trying to decide what to retrieve! He

125

ran, sniffing the air searching for the scent of a bird, but could find none. Eventually he came back and sat at my feet with tears in his eyes, thinking he had failed me. I tried in vain to explain dynamite to him, but I can't speak German. (He was a German Pointer.)

I'd like to explain something here, but you must promise not to laugh. Okay? You promised! I CAN UNDERSTAND ANIMAL TALK. There you go! You promised not to laugh.

My dog, Jed, asked me to get rid of that German. Actually, he called him "That Kraut." I really got on to him about being prejudiced, but it didn't do much good. He still went around acting superior - until I reminded him that he had been sleeping with pigs! I told him **"if I had the choice, I would rather sleep with a German any day!"** Jed and 'her Majesty' (the cat) were a real snooty pair of customers!

Anyway, I hope you haven't forgotten about the pair of grouse we left sitting in the tree! The hen looked down at the dog, and then said to her partner, "that stupid mutt is making me nervous, just standing and staring at me like that. He's been staring at me for the past five hours!"

"Well, my dear, said the rooster, "You do look especially delightful, with the moon shining down on your feathers! I can't resist staring at you either. It's making me feel a little romantic myself!"

"You may as well get that notion out of your head right now! "I've got a headache from that jerk down there eyeballing me that way. Besides, it's been a long day and I'm tired. It has always been my curse to be attractive to the opposite sex. I want to be admired for my brains and not just my body!"

"Well," the rooster replied, "If we had the brains of a crow, we'd fly out of here right now! Here comes Farmer Steve with his gun! You know how many of our children have disappeared because of that gun!"

It was at this point I stepped up and ended that conversation. Grouse are especially dumb creatures. However, in the Spring, when the males feel romantic, they are very talented at drumming. It really seems to attract the females. They forget all about brains and go for the drummer! Humans are much the same in some respects. I've seen girls on TV go ape over some goofy looking drummer. As a matter of fact, my daughter, Sandra, fell for a drummer and ended up marrying him.

Anyway, about midnight, I looked out the window and saw that dog still standing there, pointing at those two grouse. I pulled on my trousers, grabbed the gun and put the birds out of their misery!

The dog seemed grateful, and I believe his exact words were, **"Thank you Sir! Right now I'm all tuckered out, but what say in the morning we go out and hunt up a couple more grouse?"** I gave him a swift kick where he sits down!

The next winter I was working up north for Ace Explosives. A bunch of guys were sitting around the office when the conversation turned to hunting dogs. One of the men (the owner of a seismograph company) began telling us about his champion German short-haired Pointer. He explained that he had paid a thousand dollars for it, plus a lot more for having it trained. His dog had won a number of blue ribbons in competitions all across western Canada. After all that, he had the misfortune of losing it somewhere north of the town of Valleyview! He had been driving home from Yellowknife to Calgary and had stopped to rest at three a.m. Alongside the highway. He let his dog out to run. He was so tired, he fell asleep. When he awoke, the dog was nowhere to be found. After searching and calling, all to no avail, he finally gave up on ever finding him.

I spoke up and asked if he would be willing to drive twenty miles out of his way to find him? He assured me that he would drive a lot further than that, just to see him again. I informed him that his dog was at my farm at Fish Creek. He said, **"Well, how about a reward?"** So I set him straight right away!

"I couldn't afford to pay a reward, but I'd be ever so pleased if he'd just stop by and and get his dog." Under other circumstances I might have been willing to pay a little bit, but this hound had caused enough grief around our place! Judging from the strange look the owner gave me, I guess he was disappointed. But my mind was made up. I wouldn't back down!

The following week he stopped by our place. Wilma was very happy to see that Pointer go! I have to admit though, I did miss those looks of adoration he gave me when I shot a grouse for him to retrieve!

MY OWN TRAP LINE - A DREAM COME TRUE

We had been in Canada for five years when I made a trip to Edmonton to file on some homestead land. I was browsing over the maps of the country south of Grande Prairie when I noticed the area around the Kakwa River. This was facinating country; as wild and isolated as anywhere I'd heard of. I had been there previously to haul explosives to a seismograph crew and had really fallen in love with the country. It was full of wild rivers and mountains that had barely been explored. The map showed a portion outlined in red. It was right up against the western British Columbia border and amounted to almost a hundred square miles. I asked why it was outlined in red? The clerk answered that it was a registered trapline that had just come open. It was available for a five dollar registration fee. I nearly ripped my pocket getting my billfold out!

I didn't know any rich trappers, but I was going to change that!

LATER ON

I actually owned this trapline along the Kakwa, but I hadn't been able to do justice to it for a variety of reasons. Number 1: It was remote and hard to get to. Number 2: I had run out of friends who were willing to go back there as a partner and spend a winter in isolation. This was mainly due to the fact that two previous attempts had been failures, so far as money making ventures were concerned. Most of my friends had fallen for the 'matrimony theory' that claims "two can live as cheaply as one." They were now under pressure to stay home with their wives. One woman even told a story of a trapper who had run out of supplies and starved to death way back in the wilderness. His skeleton was found years later, sitting at a table still holding a note to his sweetheart. In it, he had left all his worldly goods to her. I tried to explain to my sweetheart, that as far as my worldly goods went, if you added zero to zero it still amounted to zero. At any rate, my friend's wives were telling their husbands to "stay away from that loser, Steve." If they wanted to spend a winter away from home, an oil rig paid much better wages, and they might even return home in the Spring with some money in their jeans. My wife, Wilma, had even started talking like that! I had to admit that my track record had more or less proven them right. However, this trapline dream had almost become an addiction with me. There was the remote possibility that I might even strike it rich. Everyone is allowed to have a dream. Right?

This country, being so remote, made it all the more attractive to me. I could hardly wait to get there. It was over a hundred miles from civilization and I couldn't risk taking a good vehicle in, so I bought a 1949 Ford pickup. A lot of blue smoke came from the exhaust, but as long as I kept pouring oil in, it worked pretty good.

As usual, when I had a risky adventure, I talked my friend, Arne Johnson, into joining me. It took all of five minutes to convince him that nothing could go wrong; that we'd be coming home with lots of money. Arne had some experience in trapping. I failed to mention that my only experience had come from books. That is a poor substitute for the real thing. At that time there was a seismic company working in the area of my trap line. They had plowed a trail to within ten miles from the east boundary of the line. We felt there were few obstacles remaining. We loaded up, and by dark were eating supper in a parachute tent at the end of the trail. The following day found us hiking up the Kakwa to set up camp on the trap line. We were delayed somewhat by the good squirrel hunting encountered along the way. By the time darkness set in, we had advanced only two miles toward our goal. The following days were repetitions of the first. We had a couple hundred squirrels by then. However, we found our supplies would be exhausted before Spring rolled around. So – it was back home to re-supply! Naturally, we wasted a week in town, and as fate would have it, Arne got called back to work on an oil rig! I had lost a partner and needed to find someone else. Arne's older brother, Terry, was a lot harder to convince. Especially so, since he had just gotten married a few months previously. Pauline was a better cook and much prettier than I was. However, a little begging and lure of "all that money," turned the tables in my favor! Terry was unemployed at the time so he finally agreed to head to the trap line with me. This was a real trial for him; leaving his Bride and spending at least three months in the company of dead animals and myself.

Pauline had been raised in a more sheltered atmosphere than Terry and I. I cannot imagine the pain and turmoil this venture of mine was causing her. She hid her tears from us and kissed Terry goodbye. I am surprised that we all remained good friends after that, but it just proved what a great lady she was - and still is.

I had been honored to be Terry's Best Man at their wedding. I had borrowed his car and, unknown to him, had an extra set of keys made. Their suitcases were packed and locked 'securely' in the trunk. They thought everything was safe and in control.

During the reception, some of our group unlocked the trunk

and created the usual havoc with the couple's 'unmentionables! Then, to top it all off, some ornery guys kidnaped Pauline and gave her an extended tour of both town and countryside, before returning her to her new and distraught husband! With a sigh of relief, the newly weds finally headed up the Peace River hill on the first leg of their honeymoon. It was then another unexpected event occurred. A teenage girl, Carol Spinney, had stowed away under some luggage in the back seat! It was her giggling that gave her away. So -- back into town they headed! They got rid of her and continued on their journey.

The next mishap was a broken fan belt (which I was innocent of) but nevertheless blamed for! By this time, I think Pauline had decided that with friends like this - who needs enemies! Believe it or not, we have remained the best of friends. For some reason, Terry hasn't volunteered to accompany me on any more adventures.

OFF TO THE TRAP LINE AGAIN!

There was a steep hill a few miles from the end of the trail. It was covered with about ten inches of fresh snow. We spun out before reaching the top. After four or five runs at it, the motor started knocking. We had to give up and make camp in the dark. It had turned bitterly cold (minus 40) so we didn't even bother making a fire. Instead we rolled out a large heavy tarpaulin; zipped our eiderdown bags together on half of it; crawled in and pulled the other half of the tarp up over our heads. The next morning we awoke to the sound of men's voices. I heard one say, **"I'm sure they're dead. No one could survive sleeping outdoors in this temperature!"** We felt the corner of the tarp being lifted cautiously and saw a man's face staring down at us. When I spoke to him, he jumped back and stammered, **"I thought you had frozen to death!"** We assured him we were fine, but would sure appreciate a ride up to our camp. They were glad to oblige. They told us their seismic crew would be moving out in two weeks and the trail would blow in after that.

Terry and I decided to go ahead and trap until they moved. Then we'd catch a ride out with them. Our plan had been to bring someone in to tow the pickup out for repairs. After that, we'd get in to serious trapping. We had brought a small wood stove to set up in our parachute tent. Even with the extreme cold, we managed quite well with it. We caught a good bunch of squirrels that brought about a dollar each. That at least paid our expenses!

A couple nights in a row, we were awakened by the sound of something chewing in our food supplies. We determined to put a stop to this thievery. Each time we'd hear it, we would sit up and light the lamp. But whatever it was, it would scamper away before we could see it. The snow around camp was packed so hard that the mysterious animal didn't even leave tracks. We knew it had entered our tent behind the stove. Finally one night I moved the food to the opposite side of the tent and put our bed rolls in the middle. That way, 'it' would have to go around us to escape. We left the lamp burning low and I laid my '22 rifle by my side.

Sure enough, about midnight, we awoke to the familiar sound of chewing. I quietly moved one hand to the gun and the other to the lamp. Then I sat up to shoot. As I did, something smacked me right in the face! Whatever it was, it had very cold feet! I was so startled I couldn't stifle a loud yell of alarm! Terry sat upright, laughing so hard he nearly choked. The intruder had jumped for the hole through which he had entered, only to have me sit up in direct line of his escape route. We still had no idea what the thing was! I guessed it might be a muskrat or a packrat. Whatever it's identity, it never returned! Following that episode, I found that whenever I'd be almost asleep, Terry would burst out laughing at my mishap. This continued until I threatened to leave all the cooking to him! That scared him pretty bad.

A couple weeks later we got back to Valleyview. Pauline looked so good to Terry that he refused to go back with me.

Art Adolphson, my Dad and I, returned a few weeks later to tow the pickup home. However, the roads had already drifted shut and we were forced to leave it there. Art and I were reminiscing about this not long ago. He said, **"As we stood there on the Chinook Ridge in the moonlight, we could hear the sound of the wind blowing through the pine trees. We could see fifty miles into the distance and there was not a light in sight. It seemed that we were the only people left in the world! What a lonesome feeling."**

The last I saw of that old truck was a few years later. I found it upside down, having been washed down by the Spring flooding of the Kakwa River. I abandoned it, and as far as I know, it is still there.

Leaving the Kakwa with the horses in 40 degree below weather. (Note the frost on my face.)

I am standing in waist deep snow.

A nice lynx I got.

Looking back, I have to admit that I wasn't too smart, when I consider what my choices where. Number 1: Spend the winter with a homely, bearded partner and live mostly on beans and whatever we could shoot. Number 2. Spend the winter with an attractive, twenty-three year old female and eat great home cooked meals. I'm surprised someone didn't have me committed to an institution!

The previous year, I had made a deal with an experienced trapper. He was to go in and build a cabin and trap for two years. He could keep everything he made. At that time, either I was to take over or else sell the line to him. As soon as the snow melted that Spring, a friend named Pete Flanagan and I hauled all of George G's equipment and supplies to the end of the road with plans to pack it in to where George wanted his cabin. (A distance of six miles.) There was a Big Game Outfitter, we'll call Max, who had a camp at the very end of the road. We proceeded to set up our camp near one of his corrals and planned to start first thing in the morning.

Max had pulled out the previous December so the camp was deserted, with the exception of about twenty horses he had left to winter. My friend, Pete, was a good cowboy and the the more we thought about it, the more sense it made that we "borrow" one of these horses for packing. Even better, there were some pack saddleshanging in a tree beside the corral. Having been out all winter, these horses were as wild as deer, so we made a bait of oats and hoped a few would walk in allow themselves to be trapped. When we roused ourselves the next morning, we found that the horses hadn't taken the bait, so we loaded our backpacks and headed in.

It was cool in the early morning and by nine o'clock we had worked up quite a sweat. We weren't looking forward to a full day of this kind of hard labour. George stayed to set up his camp on Baseline Lake while Pete and I headed back for another load, all the while hoping we could still snag us a horse.

Sure enough, through the trees, we could see about five horses in the corral. We sneaked in as close as we could and made a dash to slam the gate on them. They all scrambled to escape except for one which we managed to trap inside. It was a stout corral, or he too would have gotten away. He began to slam into the rails trying to dislodge them. We got a rope on him and snubbed him up short so he wouldn't cripple himself. Then the fun began. It didn't take long for us to realize that this horse had never been used, and had no intentions of starting now. I think,

133

at this point, the wisest choice would have been to turn him loose and carry everything in on our backs Neither of us wanted to admit though, that we were scared of this bronc, so we went ahead with his education. When we attempted to put a pack saddle on him, he went berserk. He tried his best to stomp us into the dirt, so we had to put him down and hobble his front feet. Then we let him up and tied a hind foot up short so we could get a pack saddle in place without committing suicide!

On the first trip, we loaded the least breakable stuff in place; then untied his hind foot and pulled the blindfold off. We ran to the fence before he realized what had happened. Boy! Did he become unglued! For the next twenty minutes we just stood back and watched the rodeo! All we were able to do, when he tried to roll on the pack, was to jump in and convince him that it was in his best interest to remain on his feet. Even then, he did his best to scrape the load off on the fence. Eventually, he wore himself down and all we had to do was convince him it was to his own advantage to follow us the next six miles in to the new camp. I admit, it was a real challenge, but with a man in front and one behind, we eventually got a good load into the campsite where George had cooked up a fine mess of stew. We were so hungry, we practically inhaled it before heading back for another load.

This horse, we named "Jughead," was slowly learning that it was useless to fight us, so the return trip went a little better. There was a wild creek we had to cross, both coming and going. It was really tempting to climb on board old Jughead, but I had to admit I was scared. Pete convinced himself that he didn't want to get crippled up so far from home, so we got a good soaking each time. The name of this creek was Lick Creek.

We got back to the corrals at about three o'clock; loaded up and headed back in. We had already done twenty four miles of hard labor and Jughead was as tired as we were. With him fairly worn out, things were going quite smoothly. We sure didn't want to battle him when he was fresh and feeling frisky! It was after dark when we arrived back at the truck, and we went straight to bed. We had put in thirty six miles since breakfast with hardly a break. This included breaking a rough bronc to the pack saddle and even to lead! We locked old Jughead in the corral overnight, just in case we needed him, but our intentions were to head for home in the morning. Both of us figured Max would be happy to have a well broke horse to use in the Fall.

The sun was just clearing the trees the next morning when we heard old George coming down the trail, talking to himself and letting out the occasional holler. He was still shaking from an encounter with a big grizzly bear just after dark the night before, and decided to call off our deal. In a quivering voice, he told us he had stayed up all night keeping the fire high and making a lot of racket. He declared, **"The whole place is swarming with Grizzlies!"** I knew there were Grizzlies around, but I also knew that "swarming" was an over-statement.

Pete and I were sore from all the unexpected exercise of the previous day, but we were sure thankful we had penned up that welll-broke horse overnight. Now we had to go back to the camp and pack everything out! Old George flatly refused to help because of his scare. We managed to pack everything out in two trips, because we had a pretty well broke horse by this time. We were actually getting a little fond of old Jughead by now. I caught Pete calling him "Sugar" when he thought I wasn't listening.

Pete and I talked it over and decided we'd throw in together next Fall and trap it ourselves. With that, we reloaded the truck; turned Jughead loose with a good feed of oats and hit the trail for home.

George had some tall tales to tell about that wild country, and the size of the bears grew with each telling! Pete and I measured the tracks where the bear that put the fun on old George. They were 14 inches from heel to the tip, and about that wide. A pretty big bear all right, but not nearly as big as he continued to grow each time George rehearsed the story!

My young bride sure looked good when we pulled in to the home place. I didn't know how I was going to break the news about next Fall's trapping plans, but I had the whole summer to think up a good story on why it was the sensible thing to do.

The next Winter, at forty degrees below zero, I was talking to myself about how stupid I was; and if I survived, I was never going to leave her for anything as dumb as a trap line again! We've now been married for 48 years (at the time of this writing) and I think I'll try to keep her for another forty eight!

MURPHY'S LAW
(As it applies to me)

Murphy's law goes something like this: "Anything that can go wrong will go wrong, and at the worst possible moment." I've noticed that it seems to apply to me on a regular basis.

There was the time Peter Flanagan and I pulled out for the trap line on a chilly November morning. We thought we were pretty well prepared with the two saddle horses and one pack horse. We had a good supply of food, axes, chain saw, and tools. The chain saw was a modern addition, as we usually had to use a swede saw. Sure, my old two ton Chevy truck was missing anything that resembled brakes, but that was only a minor inconvenience to be dealt with. We left home about midnight, so we would miss the busy traffic going through Grande Prairie.

Whenever we encountered a steep hill, all we had to do was gear down in time, and creep down in low gear. We slid quietly through Grande Prairie at about two a.m. The only inconvenience was at the traffic light in the center of town. Of course it turned red just as we came up to it! The battery was low, so the way to stop was to gear down, shut the ignition off and just at the last minute, turn the key back on. This worked well, except when we turned the key back on. The motor backfired so loudly, we were positive the police would all come running to see who was shooting a rifle on main street! This also got the horses all worked up, but we managed to escape before the police arrived. We were soon out of town, speeding along at 30 mph on our way to the trapline, which was still a hundred miles away.

It was pitch dark when we pulled down to the crossing at Stetson Creek. It was then things began to get serious. On the hill going up the other side, a water spring had broken loose and then frozen. It left a sloping hill of ice, right over the edge and some hundred feet straight down to the bottom of the creek. The only solution was to break out the axes and start chopping a track up the hill, through the overflow. In about two hours, we thought we had done enough to make it up, so we jumped in and "put the pedal to the metal!" About half way up, we began to wish we had put the chains on first! But we hadn't, and it was too late now! Of course we spun out and began sliding backwards. I felt a bit of draft as Pete bailed out, leaving me to my fate. I didn't blame him, but I will admit a lonely feeling came over me. I was considering my impending death at the bottom of the creek. Of course, I didn't die, because of a well placed rock, right on the edge of the bank. It stopped the truck just in time!

Let me tell you, it would have saved a lot of trouble had we put the chains on at the bottom instead of being perched on the edge of eternity like we were now! The horses didn't seem to appreciate it either.

However, we eventually made it over the top, and were soon tearing down the trail at about twenty mph again. About five miles from the end of the road, the temperature gauge showed the motor was over heated. We stopped and discovered the fan belt was broken. Consequently, this was where the horses were unloaded. We tried everything we could think of to make another fan belt, but nothing worked. Pete rode the horses on in to Macullah's hunting camp, while I sat in the truck waiting for the motor to cool down. I would drive awhile until it heated and then repeat the process. It had taken us about twenty hours to complete the 200 miles from home -- but we had arrived!

It was still five or six miles to my trap line, but this was the end of the driveable portion. About ten inches of fresh snow had fallen during the night, so the road out was closed (we thought). Macullah's skid trailer was locked up tight, but we were unable to overcome the temptation to break in, and jimmied the lock on a little window and crawled through. We soon had a fire going and cooked something that resembled food. With our stomachs full, we crawled into a couple bunks and were soon fast asleep. A couple hours later, we were awakened by the sound of a motor outside. We crawled out of bed, lit the lamp, and like the pair of criminals we were, awaited our fate. Of course it was Mr. Macullah, and he was a tad angry that we had broken into his shack! When we explained our predicament, and all our bad luck, he softened up a bit and forgave us.

Another reason McCullah was upset, was because he had assumed that no one would be trapping that winter, so he left a man there to trap out the beaver from an area called "Dead Horse Meadows." We didn't know this, and came on the fellow pulling a beaver out of a pond. Of course we were upset, and Pete fired a couple shots over his head with his 30.06 to let him know that we weren't pleased! He took the hint, and the last glimpse we had of him was his south end headed north! It would have taken a good horse to catch him. He seemed to think we were going to change the name of the meadow to "Dead Trapper Meadow!"

From here, we had to make four trips to pack all the supplies into camp on the trap line. On the first trip in, we set some traps along the trail and managed to catch a few martin while packing our stuff in. On the last trip, there were just a few odds and ends, including a galvanized water pail which we tied on top the pack horse's load. Just a short distance down the trail, we found a nice martin in our trap. Pete knocked it in the head and tossed it into the empty pack box and we were again on our way. Our pack horse, "Trixy," was following along about a hundred feet behind us, as Pete and I moseyed along, planning the cabin we were going to build. Suddenly we heard the water pail clanging and a strange squalling noise coming up behind us. Looking back, I saw Trixy in a dead gallop, with a terrified look on her face. Her eyes were as big as saucers and wild looking. I pulled my horse across the trail to stop her, but at the last instant I realized that she didn't even see me! I had to dig in my heels and just barely escaped being run over. The next thing we saw was Trixy's rear end going around a corner down trail -- then there was a crash and splash when she hit Lick Creek!

The bank was about fifteen feet high, and instead of following the trail, she leapt straight out and broke about three inches of ice when she hit the water. She then scrambled up on the other side. We caught up with the crazed horse about a mile up the trail. Covered with lather, her head hanging, she was totally exausted. So, Like Sherlock Holmes and Watson, we soon put the puzzle together! We discovered that instead of dying, the martin had regained consciousness and had been squalling and clawing against the sides of the pack box. This spooked Trixy. When she jumped, the water pail flew up and hit her in the head and the race was on!! The martin was making a lot of racket when Trixy flew past us, and of course the water pail swung with every jump, hitting her between the ears. Miracle of all miracles, aside from being totally winded, that good pack horse was unhurt. We made sure the martin was dead this time, and finally made it without further incident.

The next day we started our cabin and soon settled into the routine of trapping. Our cabin was 10 X 12 feet and very snug and warm. The only problem was when we were cooking we had to open the door because it got so hot in there. Most of the fur we trapped was martin, squirrel and the odd weasel.

One day, Pete and I decided to do some exploring. We took the two saddle horses and headed out in a heavy wet snowstorm. About two hours out, we came upon some fairly fresh horse tracks, which could mean only one thing. Poachers on our trap line! We took off after them, hoping to catch up to them and run them off. A little later, we found another set of tracks adjoining these. So Sherlock and Watson put their heads together and came up with the conclusion that with the heavy snow, we had been going in a big circle. The culprits we were following, were ourselves! As Pogo in the comic strip once said, "We is the enemy!"

We had eaten well on the supplies we had taken in, but as you have probably guessed -- didn't make much money. It was 40 below on Christmas morning that we packed up and headed out. The nearest settlement was about one hundred miles. We took three agonizing days before pulling into George Day's farm, located just out of Grovesdale (south of Grande Prairie). I will forever be grateful for the warm hospitality we received from these wonderful people.

Just a note here about the trail out: We had a big canvas tarp that we laid on the ground and then folded over our sleeping bags. A lot of time was taken up caring for the horses. The mornings were the worst as we repacked and saddled up. This required bare hands at minus forty, so you can imagine how hard it was.

The elder George Day was home with his daughter-in-law and grandkids. George Jr. was away logging. Mr. Day helped us care for the horses while his daughter-in-law put up a wonderful hot meal, which Pete and I almost inhaled! You may have guessed that we hadn't wasted much time cooking on the trail.

After putting away a big meal at the Day's table, she fixed up a couple beds in Grandpa Day's room, and we were set for the night. He kept us entertained late into the night with his stories. Now, about fourty years later, I still remember the stories he told us. Some of them were pretty colorful and cannot be repeated to delicate ears!

The next morning we turned our horses out with some of theirs, and Mrs. Day drove us into Grande Prairie to catch the bus to Valleyview and home. We got home just in time to travel to Oregon with Wilma. She had expected us to be gone all winter, so she was getting ready to leave.

Thus ends my last effort at trapping, and I'm not too sorry. The senior Mr. Day has now passed away, and so has the finest partner a man could ever ask for, Peter Flannagan. Pete has been gone for quite some time, and I'm still having trouble accepting it. I miss him today as much as I did then. I have been very fortunate in having good friends over the years, and I count him as one of the best.

Mr. McCullah.   My pack horse, Trixy (far right)

Art Adolphson standing by the remains of the trappers cabin built by Peter Flanagan and myself many years ago.

UNSOLVED MYSTERIES

I have done a lot of traveling on our nation's highways, both in the United States and Canada. There is a strange phenomenon that occurs over and over, and it defies description. How many times have you been driving along the highway and spotted one shoe or one boot? Not a pair - just one? How does a person lose one shoe and not the other? I know there are not that many one legged hitchhikers along our highways, so why is there never a pair?

A few years ago, Vonda Johnson (of Valleyview, Aberta), was explaining a new scientific discovery to me. It was about the difference between men and women. This was not about the obvious difference, but that either men, or else women, use only half their brain while the other sex uses both sides. Just for the sake of this mystery, let's say that women use only one half their brain. Could this be why we see so many single shoes alongside the roads? Perhaps while using the left side of their brain, they lose their right shoe and don't notice until it's too late. Or perhaps they deliberately lose one shoe, knowing full well that their good husband will buy them a new pair. We could follow this line of reasoning, except for the fact that you see an equal number of men's shoes. So that shoots down that theory! I wonder if this mystery will ever be solved. Perhaps there are some things in life that we are not supposed to understand.

Another mystery is levitation. I just finished looking this word up in the dictionary. It leaves one with the impression that this is all an illusion; that you just 'think' you saw something levitated. I would like to buy this theory, except for the fact that I personally have seen people levitated. You can laugh if you want, but it's true. I have written about this episode previously, but for the sake of this theory, I want to rehash it once more.

I was working on my chainsaw one day, shortly after Wilma and I were married. In fact, it was early enough in our marriage that she still believed that I was normal and didn't have a twisted mind. Anyway, the stubborn saw refused to start and I was really getting frustrated. Wilma walked up and innocently asked if there was anything she could do to help? I had tried all the regular proceedures to see see if the saw was getting any spark and it seemed that it wasn't. One thing I couldn't bring myself to do was to hold the spark plug wire and feel if any currant was coming through. The anticipation is usually worse than the actual occurrence. So why not have Wilma hold the wire and she could tell me if any electricity was coming through? As it turned out, she didn't have to tell me in so many words. When I cranked the saw, she levitated. Seemingly, without moving a muscle, she lifted bodily into the air to approximtely 3 feet. She hovered there for an instant before settling back to the floor. I was nearly as startled as she was, but not nearly as verbal about it! It didn't seem as much a mystery to me as it did to her! Frankly, I was struck speechless. Come to think of it, I believe I was 'struck' by something else, as well.

Back in the days when cars had points and condensers, if you were to ground the body of the condenser against the motor and hold the tip of the insulated wire on the sparkplug, it would build up voltage resulting in a strong jolt. I had just done this when my friend, Terry Johnson, came over to where I was working. I gently tossed it to him and he caught it in mid air. It happened that he touched both ends and got the full charge. Terry levitated too, just as spectacularly as Wilma had. Again, I was surprised that he could raise so high, and with so little effort! It is a true mystery. I was tempted to try it with other test subjects, but my friends began to suspect and avoid me. They didn't seem to be as interested in scientific theories as I was.

Both of these cases involved electricity, so I am inclined to think it has something to do with electro magnetic fields creating weightlessness. I'm working on some other experiments now, so I think I will leave the solving of this this mystery for a greater mind that mine.

I would like to move on to another interesting thing that I experienced personally.

When I was about ten years old we lived on a small farm outside Cody, Woming (I preferred to think of it as a ranch). I attended the Cub Scouts and enjoyed it immensely. There was one drawback to this arrangement, and that was that it took place beteen 7 and 9 p.m. The strange thing was, that I was very brave when it was daylight, but my courage seemed to evaporate after dark.

After one Scout meeting, I was walking home in the dark, expecting that at any moment, a cougar or wolf would begin to stalk me. My nerves were strung as tight as a fiddle. I was taking a short cut through a back alley on the outskirts of town. Suddenly a man stepped out of the darkness and yelled something at me. He was about fifteen feet away. I was sure he had a big knife in his hand, but I didn't linger to confirm it! I don't remember much about the first mile except the sound of the wind whipping my hair straight out behind me, and my jacket snapping in the wind. However, about halfway home I felt like I was leaning backwards instead of forward as one normally would. Looking down, I realized that my legs were outrunning my body. I was going to have to do something to reverse this process or I might fall over and be dragged along by my feet, which seemed to have a mind of their own. I had to start whirling my arms like a windmill in order to get my body caught up with my legs. By the time I noticed this phenomenon, I was going up the steep hill to our place and about to enter the yard. I almost ran right on past our house, and had to do some fancy footwork to get stopped and into the safe refuge of home. My Dad wondered why my tennis shoes were smoking, but I couldn't explain it. I didn't remember running through any fires. At this time in history, no one had beat the 'four minute mile'. Here, I, as a ten year old, had just cut the time in half and hadn't even worked up a sweat doing it! I think it is a great disaster that I wasn't clocked by an official of the Olympic committee. To think that I could actually have been famous for something! Now the world will have to remain ignorant of the 'all time fastest race' in the history of mankind! Even my normally receptive family wouldn't believe that I had just run two miles in under four minutes. I am still broken hearted after all these years. Later, I tried it from both directions and it took at least ten minutes to run the two miles.

My friend, Terry Johnson, actually flew for a short distance one day when we were in California. Terry is terrified of snakes. We were walking through a beautiful meadow, when suddenly he rose into the air and landed about twenty feet away. We were all a little puzzled over his behavior, but came to the conclusion that because it was such a beautiful heavenly day, Terry was being transported away to Heaven. Suddenly he returned to earth and began jumping around yelling something about rattlesnakes. We soon found that he had stepped on a short piece of electrical wire which had slipped up and hit him in the side of the leg. He automatically assumed he'd been bitten by a snake and decided to leave the country - but gravity refused to let him fly.

Wilma is also terrified of snakes and has been known to go completely hysterical at the sight of one - let alone being touched by one! This fear of snakes led to another unsolved mystery.

In the late 1960's, we were living in the town of Dixonville in northern Alberta. While there, we had agreed to the awesome task of being chaperones to forty young teens on a campout at Winagami Lake. As part of their program they were scheduled for a five mile hike. Wilma, another man and I were leading them from the cab of his pickup. (Don't say anything. Okay?) The other man was driving. Wilma was in the middle, and I was sitting on the passenger side with the window rolled about halfway down. Everything was peaceful, with the the sun beaming down on us. The driver reached over for his cigarette lighter and lit up a smoke. Suddenly the silence was broken by a high pitched whimper from Wilma. She lifted straight up, then dove head first out the half opened window and landed on her feet! Once on the ground, she proceeded to dance a fast paced jig outside the door.

Two amazing things had just taken place so quickly that I almost thought it must be an illusion. The evidence, however, was right before our eyes. Number one: Wilma diving head first out the window and landing on her feet; not to mention the dance, which was pretty spectacular in itself.

Number two: Her getting through the half opened window without breaking it! Now, I know exactly the size of Wilma's posterior, and there is no way she could have gotten through that small an opening without something giving! (By the way, she has perfect hips. That 1950 Chevy just had a small window!) The driver was as puzzled and shocked as I was. He asked me in a very concerned tone of voice, "Did I offend her by lighting up a cigarette?"

What neither of us knew, was that one of the kids had caught a small garter snake and put it in an empty cigarette package, which they stored underneath the truck seat. It was only a matter of time until it crawled out and slithered across Wilma's foot. The rest is history. When she was able to speak again, she told us what had happened. I suffered for my laughter later on that night inside our tent!

I was told by one of Wilma's family that her big brothers used to catch garter snakes and drop them in their little sisters britches. This may explain her strange behavior around snakes, but it doesn't explain the other unsolved mysteries.

As the television commentator would say, "If anyone has any clues to the answers to these amazing riddles, please drop me a line."

ALMOST FAMOUS ATHLETES

I have always wished I could do something in the Athletic world; something really noteworthy. But what could it be? I could see no sense in climbing into a ring with someone and trying to knock the other party unconscious. Wrestling didn't make much sense unless you were trying to take candy away from your little sister. Even then, I could just hear the crowds booing and the cat calls coming my way! So that would never make a national sport either.

For a short time, when in grade ten, I thought perhaps I had a chance. Every summer the smaller communities got together for Track Meets. It was exciting to compete against the best athletes from other schools in our district. That was, without a doubt, my best year ever. In every event I somehow managed to place in the top three. High jump: 1st place. Broad jump: 2nd place; and right near the top in all the running events. Wearing those prize ribbons, and seeing the girls casting admiring glances my way was fun. Yes, it was fun while it lasted, but I never advanced beyond the district level. I'm guessing it may have been because there were only three guys in tenth grade! You decide.

There was the time when I was nine years old and decided to run away from home. The biggest problem arose when the worst possible thing took place. The sun went down and darkness settled in. I had determined not to let panic creep in, but I soon realized I didn't have any power over emotion. The moon came up and shadows began to appear. My nerves were strung so tight I could hear my heart pounding away like a trip hammer! I was imagining all kinds of wild animals lurking about, ready to pounce on me. Suddenly a coyote howled behind me and I knew I was doomed! A great force was unleashed within me and I was gone like the wind! I heard a snapping sound coming from behind which lent wings to my feet! Later I realized it was only my shirt tails snapping in the breeze. Suddenly I saw our porch light appear in the distance. With a last great effort I slid in by our porch! I thought I was safe at last, when suddenly a dark form sped up and stopped beside me! I'm sure I was close to cardiac arrest, when I realized it was my own shadow! I had run so fast that I left my shadow behind and it had just caught up with me! The sad part of this tale is that I had broken all the world records for speed and there was no one around to time me.

When living in the Northwest Territories, I was hired to build the ice bridge across the Laird River. I didn't think the ice was safe yet and my nerves were tighter than a bow. My intuition proved correct. The ice cracked and gave way beneath my cat and me. As the cat was dropping through into the deep icy waters, a mighty rush of adrenaline set in! I did the 'broad jump' and landed running! This time there were two witnesses to the longest broad jump in history; a jump which was immediately followed by the one hundred yard dash! The problem here is that the Olymipcs have no category for the 'sitting' broad jump! Therefore my feat was not entered into the records. It seems as though my greatest achievements are lost to posterity!

The author, Patrick McMannus, has recorded a category called "The stationary panic." I have witnessed this phenomenon on more than one occasion. Let me explain his theory. A 'stationary panic' is when adrenaline sets in, and a person tries to run. However, they find that their legs, though pumping at top speed, are not moving ahead. That person can wear themselves into a hole in the ground.

One example of stationary panic happened with my Granddaughter, Tricia. We were living in a little town in Idaho called Orofino. Tricia was staying with us and attending school there. Every afternoon when she returned from school, she routinely walked from the front door to her room. She laid her books on her bed; opened her closet and hung up her coat.

I could never resist the opportunity to play a prank on my grand kids and saw the perfect chance to give her a great thrill. The following day after she left for school, I manufactured a life like dummy of a man. I put a cowboy hat on its head and stood it inside her closet. When she arrived home, she went through her regular ritual. All was silent at first -- then a loud pitched whine pierced the air! I stepped to the door and saw Tricia running in place and pointing to the closet! After she finished beating me nearly to death, with her fists, we had a good laugh about it. It was hilarious, except for my bruises!

One Saturday afternoon I was working in my shop when I suddenly heard a very fast drumming sound outside. I stepped out to find my wife running in place. Her face was chalky white and she was pointing to the woodpile where a little garter snake that was innocently sunning itself. Wilma's lips were moving but there was no sound coming out. Tricia stepped out just then and spotted the problem. She calmly walked to the woodpile and picked up the snake. She was carrying it down the road to turn it loose so the poor thing wouldn't be in such danger! Wilma's voice returned just then and she began screaming, **"Kill it! Kill it! It might come back!"**

I thought Tricia was pretty brave to pick up the snake. But would you believe that when a little bitty spider walked over her shoe, she almost went berserk! Now when she and her husband go camping, it has become part of her ritual to make poor Patrick pull the bed apart looking for spiders!

One very annoying habit Tricia had then was spending hours in the bathroom making herself beautiful. One day I was really needing to use the bathroom myself, but she was in the bathtub, leisurely reading a book. No amount of pleading would get her to speed things up. I stepped outside to find a place to end my agony and noticed a great opportunity for some excitement. I noted that the bathroom window was open. It was a fairly mild day, but there was still about a foot of heavy wet snow on the deck. Leaning against the rail, and almost beckoning to me, was a scoop shovel. Yes, you guessed it! I scooped up a shovel full of snow and heaved it through the window.

From all the commotion and screaming inside, I must have made a direct hit! She was saying something about a "ruined book and that it was impossible to have any privacy around this house....!" There was quite a bit more said, but I quickly jumped into the car and went downtown. I stopped at the restaurant and ordered Tricia's favorite take-out food. While waiting, I used their restroom! Tricia did decide to forgive me after a certain amount of groveling; and when she saw the good food.

While on the subject of pranks and practical jokes, I'd like to mention a little restaurant at Orofino called "Becky's Place." The Lady owner had a great sense of humor and had spent quite a sum of money on gimmicks for playing jokes on customers. A couple of the tables had hydraulic rams on them. A button could be pushed from the kitchen which caused the tables to rise slowly to about chin level. She also had artificial spiders that could be lowered on threads from the ceiling. This really freaked Tricia out! My personal favorite was a gadget under the seat that made a sound like someone loudly passing gas.

Wilma and I were there one afternoon when a young couple, of about seventeen years of age, came in. They were obviously enamored with each other and were sharing a banana split. The cook pressed the button from the kitchen. The result was dynamic! The girl shot out of the booth and was trying to explain that it wasn't her! Her face was beet red and her boyfriend had a stunned look on his face. I knew about this little

148

gadget so I was almost on the floor, I was laughing so hard! Then the cook buzzed it a couple more times so the girl would know she had been on the receiving end of a prank. Soon she was laughing with the rest of the crowd.

How did I get from Athletic events to all this? I think I'll quit while I'm ahead!

My cat being lifted up from the Laird River, after falling through the ice.

MARRIAGE IS BUILT ON LOVE, TRUST AND RESPECT

At the times of this writing, my wife, Wilma and I have celebrated nearly 48 years of "wedded bliss." There have been wagers made about how long Wilma could put up with me. Most have come and gone many times over. I do not understand why anyone would do this, because I know that I am easy to live with. I don't have a lot of testimonials in my possession, but I vouch that this is the truth!

I've decided that it is time I pass on to the male species, the benefit of my many years of experience on "How to achieve a lasting, loving relationship with your companion." Be prepared to take notes.

I will admit to an occasional mistake along the way, but all in all, I claim a fairly high ratio of success.

Never underestimate the strength of a sincere compliment. For example: During the first twenty years of our marriage, our only source of heat was an 'air-tight' wood heater. It was situated in the living room, near the center of the house. (Hence the term "central heating.)

Visualize the following with me: The thermometer registers forty degrees below zero. "Precious" is carrying in the evening supply of firewood. I am proud to admit that I never failed to compliment her on how beautiful she looked with her cheeks all aglow! (It is wise to overlook the ragged coat and the old wool cap she is wearing.) This little compliment from me never failed to make her eyes sparkle with pleasure! In fact, at times I saw little streaks of lightening flash from them. Often her lips were moving and I know she was murmuring 'love thoughts.' She was just too embarrassed to give them voice. I always try to be sensitive about these little tokens of affection. I've noticed that many men are not.

I can just hear the critics saying that I should have helped her carry in the wood! That is why I am still married and many of you are not! You see, early on I observed that she really enjoyed handling firewood. More than once, after filling the wood box, she would stand by my recliner and slowly caress a stick of firewood. A less observant man would probably have missed this little token of affection. You see, the satisfaction she received from a job well done gave her a warm glow of accomplishment. Today that would be termed "self esteem." I understood this even before I could spell "psychiatrist.

Another thing you might want to remember is: It never hurts to embellish the truth a smidgen on occasion - if it will make your "Honey" feel better.

Picture this: The Love of your Life gets up early to start the fire. She does this in order to melt the frost off the nailheads in the walls. Next she brings you coffee in bed. You might inform her that she brews the best cup of coffee in northern Canada! If you feel this would be stretching it a bit, you could use the term "in the entire township," or whatever you are comfortable with.

This might be a good time to remind you to NEVER .. I repeat .. NEVER compare your wife's culinary skills with that of another female - ESPECIALLY your Mother's! It is always important for her to believe she is the only woman in your life. This will insure the continuance of you being served coffee in bed. Also no one will get hurt (unless you spill your coffee!)

That reminds me of the story about a minister who was counseling a woman who was angry with her husband. The minister read her the scripture in Proverbs 25:21,22. There the writer compares showing kindness to someone who has wronged you, to "heaping coals of fire on their head." He asked her if she had ever tried this method? She replied that she had once poured hot coffee on him, but it only made matters worse!

A little enlightenment on the word "embellish" that I used previously: Some might take this to mean an untruth. Nothing is farther from the truth. Webster explains the word "embellish" as: "to adorn." I only meant it might be wise to "adorn" the truth. Thus you make the truth more attractive. As I said, "This way, no one gets hurt!"

You may be wondering what all this has to do with love, trust and respect. It should be fairly obvious by now that I love the way Wilma enjoys doing these little chores around the house. I definitely respect her right to do them as she sees fit. So let's move on to "Trust".

Trust is a very important part of any healthy relationship. Naturally, living, working and sleeping (in any kind of close quarters) requires an atmosphere of trust.

We lived for a time in the small northern town of Dixonville , Alberta. Putting up a good supply of firewood was an absolute necessity. Winters there are long and extremely cold. Allow me to digress just a moment to explain how cold it can get there. One winter the temperature fell so quickly that the mercury broke through the bottom of the thermometer. It actually raised the corner of the house (onto which it was fastened) two inches!

When you spoke to anyone during that cold spell, your words couldn't even be heard. They froze solid as they came out of your mouth. You can only imagine the difficulty in communicating! It only got worse when a chinook came in April and all those words began to thaw out! It could be very startling to be out walking and have all your previously spoken words jump out at you! By now I am sure you understand how cold it really was.

During that cold snap, I had been trying to get my McCullah chain saw started so I could cut firewood. I had been cranking on it for almost an hour with no results. I was getting more frustrated by the moment! At this point, I didn't need any firewood because I was plenty warm – almost overheated!

The lips of my twin daughters were turning blue, so I was primed for extreme measures. I had come to the conclusion that no spark was reaching the spark plugs. As fate would have it, "Sugar" appeared on the scene just then. She asked if I needed any help. Of course I needed help! The thing that came to mind was to have her hold the spark plug wire while I cranked the saw. That way we could see if there was any spark. Looking back, I realize I should have followed another course. But the results were superb. If I hadn't done it that way, I wouldn't have this to write about! As you may have guessed, things began to move along rapidly - yet almost in slow motion! I will attempt to describe the sequence of events that took place. Mere words can never do it justice, however.

A gust of air (apparently from her mouth) alerted me to look up in time to see my beloved rise about three feet in the air. She appeared to hover there for a moment.   The look of astonishment on her face alerted me to the fact that all was not going to be tranquil in our little "love nest!" Let me describe the scene this way: Her mouth resembled a large capital "O," and the sounds coming from it were not those of a happy camper! Her eyes were very large and her hair was spread out like a halo. Yet, the words she used to describe men in general (and particularly me) were not at all angelic! In fact, I didn't think it was a good description of me at all. In truth, I didn't catch all she said, because I suddenly remembered more important business outside! I do recall a buzzing sound similar to that of a UFO going past my head. It sounded a little like a hornet, but I remembered that the hornets had all had the good sense to freeze to death!

I want to insert a little advise here. DO NOT TELL YOUR WIFE HOW BEAUTIFUL SHE IS WHEN SHE IS ANGRY! It only seems to increase their anger. Come to think of it, we never were able to find my favorite coffee cup after this! (Someone must have stolen it.)

I then proceeded to cut wood with a dull swede saw for about an hour. I split an armful and carried it in. Then I went back for a bucket of drinking water. At this time I felt that an apology was in order. Strangely enough, she didn't have one! So, I set the example. About half way through my apology, a vision of her leaping into the air came to me. I began to laugh! (Normally NOT a good idea.) She began to laugh and soon we were both laughing hysterically and all was forgiven. You will notice, I didn't say "forgotten!" To this day she won't even touch a dipstick if I ask her to!

So much for "Trust!" But two out of three ain't bad!

In closing, I want to leave you with a quote: "A good sense of humor will cover a multitude of sins." Steve 2:3 (Lusch version)

About The Author

The Author, Stephen Allen Lusch, was born on Nobember 2, 1937 to William and Esther Lusch. He was the only son of the four Lusch siblings. From almost 'day one' wherever this modern day "Tom Sawyer" went, Mysterious, unusual and exciting things transpired!

Steve and his wife, Wilma Fern (nee Miller) are now retired and living happily at Valleyview, Alberta. A repeat of Steve's parents, he and Wilma are also the parents of one son and three daughters! Their Grandchildren number twelve and Great Grandchildren total six.

ISBN 142515877-3

9 781425 158774